DAWN

EVEN
Still

The Journey From
BETRAYAL to
FORGIVENESS
and **REDEMPTION**

First Print Edition, 2024

Printed in China

Publishing Services: Jodi Cowles, Brandon Janous, and Rachael Mitchell (Blue Hat Publishing)
Cover Design: Tim Marshall (Blue Hat Publishing)
Interior Layout: Jodi Cowles (Blue Hat Publishing)

ISBN (print): 978-1-962674-31-7
ISBN (ebook): 978-1-962674-32-4

While the author has made every effort to provide accurate information at the time of publication, neither the publisher nor the author assumes any responsibility for errors or changes that occur after publication.

Unless otherwise noted, all Scripture quotations are taken from the Christian Standard Bible® (CSB). Copyright © 2017 by Holman Bible Publishers. Used by permission. All rights reserved.

Where notated, Scripture quotations are taken from the Holman Christian Standard Bible® (HCSB). Copyright © 1999, 2000, 2002, 2003, 2009 by Holman Bible Publishers. Used by permission. All rights reserved.

BLUE HAT
PUBLISHING
BOISE · KNOXVILLE · NASHVILLE · SEATTLE
WWW.BLUEHATPUBLISHING.COM

Contents

To the one reading this, may you find the love, compassion, and grace that are woven through these pages, and may you see it for what it is, the heart of Jesus.

Foreword

As I watched Dawn sit with her face buried in her hands, sobbing quietly, shoulders moving in rhythm with the tremendous pain rising up from her, my heart was torn. Not a word was spoken, and yet her body so clearly communicated the shame, loss, disbelief, fear, and questions of how she had gotten here. Her choices had led to this horrible harvest. I did not need to know all the intricacies of the pit in which she had found herself to see that she was broken and desperate and stripped of the faith that could tell her she would be okay—more than okay—that God was faithful and would walk beside her on this incredibly dark and difficult path and would bring the healing and hope promised.

Compassion poured out and together we wept, begging for help from our Father. And in those first moments, and the days to come, I was witness to the kind, patient, tender care of our meek and lowly Savior, tending to the enemy-cultivated, self-inflicted wounds of this woman, her marriage, and her faith. Grace and mercies poured out from His loving hand.

If you find yourself in a similar narrative—or maybe one that is far different, but the gnawing aching of a seemingly impossible situation is all too familiar—this story will be a lifeline for you. If the loudest voice in your head condemns and screams "Unforgivable," and the life-sucking pain in your heart is paralyzing, this book will be a balm for your soul. This story—one of God's miraculous, hope-filled stories—illustrates the reality of the need for repentance, the indescribable gift of redemption, and the miraculous act of restoration. And regardless of the place you find yourself in, rescue is offered—cloaked in love, forgiveness, and the promise of hope.

Over and over in God's Word, we see impossible situations where the Creator Almighty transforms and brings life where nothing but death, darkness, and emptiness reigned. He is the God of the possible. He is the One who knows you, sees your brokenness, and has a purpose for the overwhelming destructive places in which we abide. He is the one who brings fragrance and beauty when all seems too far gone. He wastes nothing. He redeems all.

Dawn and Jeremy have lived out an incredibly difficult part of their marriage and have borne a few scars. Although bad days—many of them overwhelming—have flipped by on the refrigerator calendar, the eternal weight of glory has stepped out of *chronos* time into a healing that is eternal. Through their hardships and pain, they have found hope and joy as our faithful Lord renewed their minds and hearts and their deep love and commitment to each other.

If you were to let Dawn brew you some extra-sweet iced tea—the only way to enjoy it—eat some of her delicious maple cookies, and sit awhile with her on the porch, you would find yourself with side-aches from laughing, mascara running, and your face hurting. She is so full of joy and perspectives that seem to come right out of Heaven, with a little spit and fire added for good measure. Her way of looking at situations is clear and unencumbered by the dross of what used to be or what's been done.

She sets her face like flint, focused on the transformational message of a life changed and sustained by grace so enormous we cannot begin to hold it in our universe. She loves big. She can now. Dawn has experienced a life-changing walk with the Lord. He has exploded her heart to reach out to hurting people when the enemy prowls about to whisper lies of deceit, distraction, and discouragement. She holds fast and believes this truth way down in the depths of her rescued self: This freedom is also for you and for me.

She is a passionate image-bearer who proclaims the joy of living out the priceless gospel day after day, person to person, until we look on the face of the One who gives us hope . . . even still.

LaGaye MacDowall, Friend and Mentor
Director of Church Care and Counseling Ministry

Preface

We all sin, and the church is a place where sinners are welcome, but we don't always act that way. Too often we leave people to deal with the consequences of their sin alone or in secret, or we treat them as though their sin is unforgivable. Neither of these is the way of Jesus. This is a story of how I experienced restoration from God, my church, my family, and my friends after I made some awful choices ten years ago. It's a story of how *you* can also be restored, no matter what you've done. It's a story of how the church can show mercy and grace to anyone and everyone. It's a story of God's redemptive love.

Glory in the Rescue

Chapter One

The Slumber of Sin

I jumped as his knuckles hit the table and split open. Blood began to pour out from his hand, seeping into the grains of wood on the table as tears fell from his eyes. This kind and gentle man with the most tender heart, the man I'd happily married thirteen years before, had just been faced with words no one wants to hear. I sat there frozen, stunned, unable to believe the words that had just come out of my own mouth. I had not wanted to tell him, but I had no choice, it was coming out. I was going to be exposed. I just kept thinking, *This can't be my life. I didn't really do this, did I?* Yes, yes I did. I did it. I made the choice. As these words of confession filled the air, Jeremy came undone. Life as he knew it was gone, ruined, done. His knuckles bled, his eyes wept, and his heart broke.

All my life, I had wanted that fairytale dream. You know, the one where you find the perfect mate, you live in the flawlessly decorated farmhouse, and you have two beautiful babes that make your Instagram feed the envy of all. The one where love is always perfect with your mate, you are completely fulfilled, and raising your kiddos is all things playdough, playdates, and chocolate-sprinkled doughnuts.

Even when I had a wonderful husband and two precious children, there was still a void, a gaping hole in my soul where I desperately wanted more. Sure, sometimes my husband brought home my favorite ice cream on a day when I thought exhaustion couldn't be any crueler, but other times he got on my last nerve when he forgot to take out the trash again. It was often a messy house, with dishes piled up and poopy diapers, and sometimes the poop went further than the diaper. It was often sleepless nights, stretching paychecks, and barely scraping by. This just didn't seem fun, didn't feel good, and definitely was not the fairytale lifestyle I had dreamed of and so desperately wanted.

I began feeling like I was living a miserable life. This left me empty, void of any contentment or wholeness. I spent countless days wondering what was still out there that could truly make me happy. I was chasing that feeling of completion and satisfaction, feverishly craving the accolades and praise of those around me. And in my desperation, I would do anything and everything necessary to get it.

Years into living in sheer emptiness, I began working in ministry on staff at a large church. This catapulted me into the spotlight: I got accolades, friends came easily, and foes didn't matter because it seemed like I finally had it all. Add to this the fact that I worked alongside my best friend's husband, someone who was adored by the masses and who in turn was giving me praises—that was the icing on the cake.

My husband and I had become fast friends with this couple, a friendship blooming from a chance encounter orchestrated by God. We spent birthdays together, enjoyed holiday gatherings and vacations—we all simply enjoyed doing life together. At the church, this man and I were a dynamic duo who worked side by side on many projects in addition to the out-of-office friendship the four of us had. I felt as though, at last, I had reached paradise.

Then one summer day, two souls began to link that should never have connected, while four lives began to break before they ever even realized they were broken. A simple conversation between me and my best friend's husband turned into an hours-long chat, late into the night. Two hearts exposed more than ever should be exposed, opening the way to a path that should never be journeyed. It was a slippery slope leading to deep, dangerous waters. The enemy had a toehold.

I reasoned away that inappropriate conversation. *It's simply two people, close friends, it's no big deal. No one needs to know because nothing will ever come of it.* Over the next several months, lines were crossed and lives decayed as the toehold turned into a foothold. One text turned into five, which turned into phone conversations, which evolved into long chats at the coffee shop over a French press. As I rationalized every thought and act, that foothold became a stronghold. Validating all of our movements became easy, and everything seemed acceptable in my eyes. Eventually, my guard came down completely, and any voice of reason fully escaped me. I did things I never thought I'd do and went to places I never thought I'd go.

Somehow, in my deceived mind, everything was fine. It felt so good and so right, so surely it must be acceptable. I found myself telling someone who wasn't my spouse that I loved him, and I was totally taken by the fact that he was telling me the same in return. I found myself planning a life together with him, and it seemed magical, like the fairytales in the movies. I found it easy to believe that somehow the Lord would see this through because we were meant to be together, so He would indeed work it out for our good!

He and I took a ministry trip alongside a team of faithful people serving the Lord to feed the souls and bellies of hungry children. The mission field, a place so sacred in the heart of God, became a vacation spot for sin. While we hid under the guise of serving the Lord so well, the two of us shamefully sought ways we could spend time together while we were away from our families in a foreign country. Instead of feeding the starving bellies of those precious children, I was feeding the selfish desires of my mangled and empty heart.

My body was the first to say no. Living this fraudulent lifestyle, this sinful paradise, destroyed me physically. Over the duration of the affair, my body melted away, a diet I don't recommend. As I convinced myself this was bliss, my body signaled otherwise. At mealtime, my body rejected anything I tried to put in it, and when questioned about the drastic weight loss and lack of appetite, I made whatever excuse sounded plausible at the moment. But still I persisted in this affair.

Let me acknowledge that I now recognize that the logic I used to justify my behavior was irrational and outrageous. To that I say: This is what happens when we turn the focus from God to ourselves. My thinking was scary, twisted, and warped. I was blinded, depleted, and desperate. When emptiness lingers in our souls, our hearts and minds become vulnerable to anything that will make us feel good in the moment. Emptiness takes residence when we choose not to allow God to fill the blank spaces in our hearts.

With the empty abyss I existed in, my number one priority had become making myself feel good, and seeking the happiness I was missing.

In order to accomplish that, my boundaries disappeared faster than the chips and salsa at a Mexican restaurant. And my priorities changed to accommodate.

It was an alarming, disillusioned place to live, but welcome to the mind of sin justified. When you are in the depths of sin, the pit of false bliss, you are empty, irrational, and reckless. It is frightening how good the enemy is at planting little seeds of doubt while growing the roots of deception. Even as believers doing ministry work, hearts can become entangled when boundaries are ignored and priorities are distorted. Evil spreads itself through every open door, basking in the glory of deception. I believe one of the enemy's greatest accomplishments is realized when he has seeped into the trappings of ministry, causing us to be guilty of fraud to the highest degree: a victory he will stop at nothing to achieve.

We can appear to have it all together, and all the while our insides are wretched and worn from a soul that is slowly succumbing to the bellows of the evil one. It is as though he is sitting at his vessel of fire, stirring the flames and igniting the blazes of destruction. He smiles at this small victory he thinks he has won. We are so ensnared in his grip that the cries of our desperate hearts are drowned out by the approval of others—and as long as the affirmations roll in, the façade will stand. It's a cycle we are constantly managing, never knowing when the pieces we are juggling to maintain appearances will slowly start to drop, and life will begin to crash down one shattered piece at a time. All the while, the evil one just keeps watching and stirring, savoring the glories of his bedlam.

The depths of sin are a dark, lonely place, yet they carry a space of disillusionment where you feel satisfied, free, and happy. This space is only gratifying for a brief, fleeting moment. That brief moment leads us to perilous places where hearts are broken, lives are mangled, and relationships are fractured. There is no truer descriptor for sin than a quote that saturates the internet and many Sunday sermons: "Sin will take you farther than you ever expected to go; it will keep you longer than you ever intended to stay, and cost you more than you ever expected to pay."

Sin takes you farther than you want to go because you have stepped away from the light of a Savior into the blind pits of darkness. Before you know it, you turn to your reflection and do not recognize the person staring back at you. Once you have reached that place, it can seem like you are stuck there, wallowing in the lie that hope has been lost forever, a feeling that paralyzes you to keep you there longer than you ever wanted to stay. It keeps you long past that period of momentary bliss to the place where you begin to wake up from the slumber of sin wondering, *how did I get here?* You wake to a debt that seems insurmountable, that sin costing more than you ever really had in your account.

But the insides of a soul in turmoil cannot stay hidden. Sin makes itself evident in every facet of our lives no matter how hard we try to conceal it. Eventually, concealing sin becomes impossible, and it advances to the final round of destruction, which is usually exposure.

For me, it had been brewing for several months: that moment of exposure where my secrets were going to burst. I believe that deep inside, I knew it would eventually happen. However, with that place of clarity completely covered in the sludge of sin, it was impossible for me to truly realize or even dare to recognize this inevitability. Then the day finally came when the bomb exploded and the shrapnel soared. There I stood, fully exposed and defeated, hurting everyone I loved. There they stood, fully betrayed and heartbroken, left to pick up the pieces.

Including my husband in the kitchen.

Although I didn't see it then, in my husband I really *did* have my Prince Charming whom the Lord created perfectly for me. He isn't perfect, but neither am I. I am certain that Jesus is the only perfect thing about a relationship. I also had my two beautiful babes whom the Lord so perfectly wove into our lives at just the right time, even if it wasn't always playdough, playdates, and chocolate-sprinkled doughnuts.

Would I lose them? Would I lose everything?

When I woke up from the slumber of sin, I was unable to look at myself, unable to recognize the girl in the mirror. I did not want to acknowledge the person I had become, the one who had betrayed so many, because I felt somehow as though I'd also betrayed myself and the person I thought I was. The person I thought I was would never have betrayed her spouse, her family and friends, or her church. The person I thought I was would never have poured out the pain and agony that those around me were now engulfed in because of my choices. How would I even begin to say I was sorry? How could anyone even look at me? How could people ever trust me again? Maybe they never would.

Or maybe, just maybe, I would be loved . . . even still.

Chapter Two

The Shrapnel of Sin

S in explodes like the shrapnel of a detonated bomb, its fragments piercing everything within its reach. It is so harmful that it can kill a soul as quickly as it can stop a heart. This may seem dramatic, but it is the absolute truth. Our sins and the choices we make, can have deep, devastating effects on others just as much as they devastate us.

I can still remember the wails that came from my husband as the pain cut so deep that the only thing he could do was weep. There was a day he couldn't even get up off the bathroom floor because the anguish of what I'd done had paralyzed him. To hear the soul-crushing sobs of my husband while he lay there paralyzed was a jarring visualization of what I had done. I lay beside him, barely able to look at him, knowing I was what had put him in this state. Yet at the same time, I was trying to comfort him. It was a duality of worlds where the closest person to me was in so much pain and needed me the most, yet we were the furthest apart we'd ever been because I was the source of said pain. It is something I never in my life want to experience again.

For several days after the confession, hours upon hours were spent admitting everything, sharing the ugly, awful, nitty-gritty details. These hours were filled with excruciating questions that only had unpleasant answers. The anguish of that process is like no other. I was at a crossroads of confession, peering into the eyes of the one I'd hurt the most, and it did indeed awaken me from the slumber of my sin. On one hand, I didn't want to confess it all for fear that it might hurt him so deeply that forgiveness would never come. Yet, on the other hand, when it's time to confess, the most bold and humble thing one can do is step fully into the honesty of your mess and empty every single bit of it out.

Imagine being in your garden, seeing the weeds overtaking the beauty of the blooming flowers. If you don't pull that weed out at its root, getting every single bit of it, it will spread like wildfire and choke out the beauty, killing everything around it. When we don't empty sin out by confession, every bit of it, it will seep into every part of our being and kill our souls.

As the days continued, layers were peeled, the word got out, and things went public. My choices cost me countless friendships. They cost me my job. They completely cost me the trust of everyone I knew. I could write another book on all of the devastation that came from this story. Sadly, that is the inevitable, ugly consequence of sin.

Many of our closest friends walked away from both Jeremy and me when I stood fully exposed before the crowd that had formed. It was too much for them to bear, but others stood in the fire with us ready to battle in whatever way it took.

I can still see the heartbreak on the faces of our friends and family. Each time I had to confess, it was despair, over and over and over. Those near and dear would start with looks of confusion, and then came absolute anguish. They would look at me as though they were trying to figure out who I was, as if everything they had ever known about me was a lie and I was the image of evil who was confessing to them. How could I blame them for questioning everything about me as they heard the despicable things I had done?

I didn't, I couldn't.

More news spread, more hearts were impacted, more tears were shed, and more questions mounted. Cue the rampant rumor mill, the next piece of shrapnel to hit.

When you find yourself in a situation where bad choices are exposed, it detonates the eruption of chatter, enabling anything and everything to be said and believed about you. You can't defend it, you can't deny it, the only thing you can do is sit back and let it happen. It is another facet of the painful surrender that has to happen upon waking from that slumber of sin. I tried to rise and defend myself against the untrue things spoken. Everything in me wanted to go line by line, shouting out, "That's not true!" but it was pointless. No one would hear me, and no one would believe me, because all anyone saw was a cheater, betrayer, and liar. Some of the things I heard said about me were shocking. However, I simply had to let them be said, because trust was broken and anything I wanted to say in opposition would be doubted.

Aspects of the truth were woven into the lies, which made it all the more twisted and mind-blowing. It was a free-for-all, and trying to defend against anything was like trying to play whack-a-mole at the arcade.

While I attempted to squash one trail of lies, another popped up beside it, over and over. Sadly, most of this was being done by Christians.

It was exhausting. There were days when I just wept with weariness, thinking my life was over, there was no coming back from this, people would never trust anything I said or did again and this rumor mill would never stop grinding. Another wave of rumors would break like another line of waves in the ocean. Just when I would think it was quiet and the coast was clear, another wave rolled in and knocked me down, taking my breath away—relentless attacks that, in the moment, I thought I deserved.

A woman who was only an acquaintance when the scandal hit was strolling through the grocery store with her son and husband. It was actually the day that everything was revealed, and she had no idea yet. While she was in the store, a woman who also attended our church scurried up to her with a smile on her face, giddy to share the breaking news. After hearing the news, she went home with a pit in her stomach, brokenhearted for me. She didn't call the next friend to share the news; she didn't laugh or think of something else about me she could share with the next listening ear; she grieved. Right then she prayed and asked God how she could help. As far as she was concerned, the rumor mill stopped with her. The shrapnel was laid to rest at her doorstep, and she didn't want to throw it any further.

I can tell you now, the rumor mill will always be undeserved. It is not right or moral no matter what has happened, no matter the circumstances. Most importantly, it is sinful and does not honor our God. Sin plus sin doesn't equal right. However, let's be real; even though it isn't right, it is a consequence of our actions. But just as my friend did, when the rumor mill comes around to you, be the bigger person, honor the Lord, and don't keep it going. Instead, shut it down.

Have you ever heard the phrase "Live above reproach?" It is found in scripture several times. One example is 1 Timothy 3:2, which says, "An overseer, therefore, must be *above reproach*, the husband of one wife, self-controlled, sensible, respectable, hospitable, an able teacher" (HCSB).

I fully grasped what this meant as I endured the lies being spoken. You see, when you're living above reproach, untruths spoken about you will be hard for others to believe. The weight of truth will be on your side instead of the side of the gossip. However, when trust is broken and you are guilty in the first degree, people will believe whatever is put out there. It was honestly astounding, the lengths people went to with lies and stories. To this day, ten years later, some still believe some of the things that were said.

When we choose to be disobedient, lacking integrity in our lives, and bend even just a little bit on anything, living above reproach quickly falls away.

Here is the thing: In the past, anytime a scandal broke out, I was the first to rule in favor of a guilty verdict whenever I heard the latest gossip or watched the latest outrage hit. The juicier it got, the more I believed, and the harder I judged whoever was at fault. My mind went wild with the "how-could-theys" and the "are they even a Christian" insults. Heck, I would even go so far as to say, "Is their entire life a lie?" That is, until it was me in the middle of the scandal and the topic of every watercooler conversation. It brought a great humbling to my heart and soul that I wouldn't wish upon anyone.

Listen, if you remember nothing else from this book, remember this: Please, for the love of all that is holy, do not believe everything you hear about someone, and I beg of you, don't think you must repeat it. When you hear of the latest scandal or fall from grace, grieve for that person, pray for that person, and maybe, just maybe, encourage that person. May the last thing you even think about doing is feed the fire of gossip.

Another piece of shrapnel that sin throws at you is broken trust, which in reality is a branch of the rumor mill. It was hard to process the fact that every single thing I said and did at this point was called into question. I had been tried and convicted, guilty of everything. Broken trust is a massive consequence, and that trust can take months and sometimes years to build up again.

Jeremy questioned everything I did, everything I said, and everywhere I went. Why wouldn't he? I had ultimately betrayed him in all of those areas for months. It was his prerogative to do this and mine to oblige. If he had questions, I answered with more details than were necessary because the fight was on to earn his trust back. Gaining back his faith in me was my job, my battle to fight, and my victory to win.

When it comes out that you lied about something as simple as a trip to the grocery store, it takes a long time to earn back the belief that you are simply going to the grocery store. In a marriage, those should be assumed truths, until they aren't. Earning back that trust meant providing proof. It meant Jeremy picking up my phone at any point to simply look through, or opening my computer to do the same. For Jeremy, this was just as painful as it was for me. He had no desire to have to look through stuff, comb through my phone, or check my whereabouts. Yet, to gain his confidence back, those were the things he had to do for a time, and I had to let it happen.

For others, like friends and family, it was about honest, open conversations with them, noticeable humility and brokenness in me, and many, many accountability meetings. It was the willingness to take the doubts and the questionable looks and acknowledge their disbelief in me as I slowly but surely built back their trust.

It didn't come fast for anyone, and it didn't come easy. Broken trust builds barriers that have to be broken down by evident, humble, full-surrender transformation. This only happens with the help of the Holy Spirit being made alive in you while all the junk and mess is emptied out of you.

The shrapnel is messy and creates deep and excruciating wounds. It is the aftermath that no one wants to talk about or acknowledge, when the temptations are dancing in front of you. It is the repercussions that the enemy wants you blinded by when he is dangling the falsities of satisfaction and fulfillment. The enemy's guarantee of serenity is the beginning of an assured catastrophe in your life.

Before my affair took on a life of its own, there were many justifications and complete denial that anything bad would happen on the other side. These are the depths Satan will go to to twist your reality so that you buy into what he is selling. That first late-night phone call that no one knew about left me giddy. It didn't leave me worried someone would find out. That first "I love you" from a man who was not my husband, but instead my best friend's husband, left me feeling like I was in a Hallmark movie. I wasn't worried it would end up causing the deepest pain possible for Jeremy and my best friend when they read those messages months later. That first embrace with that man felt like nothing I had ever felt, the dreamiest of times, and something I had waited all my life for—not the beginning of the most destructive year of my life, the worst thing I could ever do, or the next step in a completely inappropriate relationship. Never mind that I had the most incredible man there ever was waiting on me at home. I had bought into the lie that he wasn't good enough. I had justified to myself that there was something better.

The paragraph above probably leaves your stomach in knots because such twisted rationalization is repulsive. Hear me when I tell you: This is what sin does. This is the delusion that evil has the capacity to create, a ticking time bomb whose aftermath of pain, heartache, and broken trust is never truly understood until it explodes.

If only living like our Savior stayed at the forefront of our minds, we'd avoid a lot of heartache and heartbreak. Others-centered, selfless, kingdom-minded living brings out the best in us. Instead, we often choose self-centered, selfish, worldly-minded living, which brings out the worst. Why do we do this?

We do this because of our flesh. Our sinful, human nature. Every single one of us has a void, a deep-rooted, soul-hungry, heart-aching void. That void seems easy to fill with quick and cheap things. You know, the good, greasy McDonald's cheeseburger, or the burrito and taco combo at Taco Bell that quickly fulfills that junk food craving? Then a few hours later, you feel like trash, your stomach is in shambles, and you question why you ever thought that would satisfy the hunger you had. The same goes for the quick fixes to the soul void we have. When we try to fill it with earthly things, sinful things, we end up feeling like trash, our life in shambles, and we question every decision we ever made.

In one way or another, we have all been there. Maybe you are there right now. You filled that void with temporary things and now find yourself sitting in the aftermath, wondering how the heck you're going to make it out.

Don't stop now, friend; there is hope on the other side. There is a rescuer who comes with the goodness of grace to mend our wounds with his healing hope.

Chapter Three

The Savior of Sin

I was forced to confess to Jeremy. It was going to be exposed and if I didn't tell him he was going to find out anyway. When I admitted everything to him, it wasn't out of deep remorse or conviction, it was out of necessity and self-preservation. The brokenness and the full realization of what I had done took a few days to catch up.

I remember the very moment I realized the depravity of my sin. It was just days after my world exploded, and I was standing in the shower, sobbing, overcome with the horror of my situation. My life was over, my world was shattered, and I had destroyed every single part of it. As this thought consumed me, the sobs grew stronger and stronger, and the angst grew deeper and deeper. Taking a breath felt like a thousand rocks were sitting on my chest, taking every ounce of my being to lift. I became so burdened that I collapsed in the shower, sliding down the wall into a puddle, while the shower just kept pouring water down over me. All the while, guilt and shame were raging in my soul. A metaphor if I'd ever seen one: the water continually pouring out over me, and me hardly able to take a breath as my insides drowned in sorrow. Weeping, in pain, not wanting to move from this place, I pleaded with the Lord for rescue. I was so overcome that all that would come out of my mouth was a whisper for help. "Help me." "Save me." I even just asked Him to "take me" at that moment. For a fleeting second, I thought it would be better for everyone if I was just gone. If they never had to see me, to face me, it would be easier to heal and move on. While I don't believe I was ever suicidal, that was a moment of wanting Him to simply take me, an ending not by my own hand but by His.

The water kept coming, the sobs kept flowing, and my pleas for help continued. I could not even comprehend what to do next. Even just stepping out of the shower seemed impossible. It was a moment of absolute darkness, total hopelessness, and complete brokenness. It was the moment I knew there was no way that on my own, by my strength, I could get out of this, move forward, or make my life whole again.

My mind raced in circles, round and round from memory to memory of all I had done. I couldn't escape them. I didn't want to remember those things right then, but I couldn't stop the memories from coming. I didn't want to see the eyes of the man I'd created secrets with. I didn't want to remember the lies I'd told. I didn't want to think about the text messages I had sent. *Please, Lord, take it all away,* I begged, pleading with Him to let these flashes of memories fade. I was paralyzed.

And then, it began to happen. The collision of hopelessness meeting hope, war meeting peace. There, in the middle of it all, the whisper of surrender seeped out of my mouth. "I need You, God." That moment became a miraculous encounter. The shower became a sacred space. The

Lord lifted me, and I heard Him speak back to me that He would indeed rescue me. I knew right then with everything in me that He would. I felt the presence of the Lord take hold of me in that space, and the rescue began. It was a supernatural encounter. I truly felt as though the Lord was right there with me, holding me tightly in a warm embrace of comfort.

Our good and gracious Redeemer could have stopped right there. That was all I needed in that marvelous encounter. But in His magnificence, He didn't, because He is just that good and tender and compassionate. He sent a physical reminder and reassurance. The very next minute, my incredible husband, who had heard my wails, came rushing in. Despite his own deep pain and heartache, he came and held my weeping, broken body and said to me, "We are going to make it."

We cried together, tears streaming down from our eyes as the shower continued to mimic us. He held me as I clung to him, and brokenness bloomed right there. This very moment assured him and me both that God was with us, and He would make us new.

As I write these words, my eyes well up ten years later at the beauty of that encounter. Isn't it just like our God to do that? Using a man who had just had his world shattered by me, and enabling him to look beyond his own agony to hold and comfort me, the very person who caused his pain. It was a moment that could only point to the glory of our God because no one in their humanness could ever do that. This was one of those moments where the Lord showed His grandeur in the midst of a mess, a sweet glimpse of His promise to rescue, a foretaste of His mercies, and a declaration of grace.

The mercy of God withholds the punishment we deserve. (Side note: The consequences of our actions and God's punishment are distinctly different.) What I deserved that day was my husband ignoring my cries or coming in and telling me to get up and get ahold of myself. He could have very easily just said, "This is what you get," and walked away. He did not. God in all his wonder, used him in the rescue.

The grace of our God gives oxygen to hope in devastation. Because of Jeremy's faith, he was given the grace of our God to endure that moment with me, and I was given the grace of God through his actions. What happened in the shower that day was both His grace and mercy being lived out through the heart and soul of my husband.

God, in His rescue, sustains us in love, compassion, patience, and a whole lot of grace. In scripture He tells us that grace is all we need. It is sufficient. It is the only thing needed upon your surrender.

In the shower, full awareness of all I had done came over me. As awareness arose, so did the cry for help. Jesus Christ is waiting when we wake up from our depravity, coming to our senses, and He is the one who will resuscitate our souls.

Realizing our need for rescue from sin means owning our mess, confessing our mess, and then surrendering to let Him work in us. There is a passage of scripture that clearly lays this process out, giving an excellent example of the well of grief we can find ourselves in that turns into the fountain of rescue from our Deliverer. Psalm 51 is one of the most famous Psalms, and it discusses sin, guilt, confession, and forgiveness. It is where King David felt the conviction of his sin and then cried out for rescue. Let these words wash over you as you read them:

Be gracious to me, God, according to your faithful love; according to your abundant compassion, blot out my rebellion. Completely wash away my guilt and cleanse me from my sin. For I am conscious of my rebellion, and my sin is always before me. Against you—you alone—I have sinned and done this evil in your sight. So you are right when you pass sentence; you are blameless when you judge. Indeed, I was guilty when I was born; I was sinful when my mother conceived me.

Surely you desire integrity in the inner self, and you teach me wisdom deep within. Purify me with hyssop, and I will be clean; wash me, and I will be whiter than snow. Let me hear joy and gladness; let the bones you have crushed rejoice. Turn your face away from my sins and blot out all my guilt.

God, create a clean heart for me and renew a steadfast spirit within me. Do not banish me from your presence or take your Holy Spirit from me. Restore the joy of your salvation to me, and sustain me by giving me a willing spirit. Then I will teach the rebellious your ways, and sinners will return to you.

Save me from the guilt of bloodshed, God—God of my salvation—and my tongue will sing of your righteousness. Lord, open my lips, and my mouth will declare your praise. You do not want a sacrifice, or I would give it; you are not pleased with a burnt offering. The sacrifice pleasing to God is a broken spirit. You will not despise a broken and humbled heart, God.

In your good pleasure, cause Zion to prosper; build the walls of Jerusalem. Then you will delight in righteous sacrifices, whole burnt offerings; then bulls will be offered on your altar. (Psalm 51)

You can see where David doesn't try to diminish what he's done, he owns it! Pay special attention to the first paragraph, where he identifies that it is against our God and Him alone that he has sinned. Another part of the realization is what sin boils down to every single time: It is acting directly against our God. David owns it and then begins to ask for rescue. He asks for cleansing, renewal, and restoration. He also says here that the sacrifice pleasing to God is a broken spirit. Simply bringing our brokenness opens the door to Him bringing His rescue.

In fact, I believe God began the rescue before I ever even asked for it. He exposed my affair and pulled me out of that pit before I ever wanted to be saved. I think that if I had jumped right back into the depths of sin after that, it would have been a different story. But I woke up, I looked at myself in the mirror, and I broke. I began to plead for help, asking for rescue, asking to be cleansed, and so the rescue mission for my heart and soul continued.

The thing that amazes me the most about it all is that He didn't have to rescue me. He didn't have to choose to pull me out. He didn't have to fight for me. But He did.

He could have left me wallowing in my sin. He could have left me floundering until I did indeed lose it all. He could have left me going deeper and deeper into a wretched state of despair. But He didn't.

In my place of brokenness, I came to that realization, and it was humbling. I fully grasped the sinful, shameful state of my life, indulging in worldly pleasures to a degree so corrupt I betrayed the nearest and dearest to my heart, all while proclaiming the name of Christ. Yet still, there He was to rescue me. Talk about a bring-you-to-your-knees moment.

Or rather for me, bringing me to the floor of my shower. Oh, what a Savior, the Alpha and Omega, the Almighty, that He would deliver me! And He didn't stop there.

Glory in the Restoration

Chapter Four

The One Who Means the Most

A Chapter From Jeremy

Forgiveness is something I have always felt I've been able to do pretty easily. It was the way I was raised, and then, coming to know the Lord, I knew that I needed to forgive people because I was forgiven through Jesus Christ. Going through the beginning of this hard journey, this was something that I truly had to rely on to make it through the day sometimes. The pain and heartbreak that I went through are something I don't wish on my worst enemy.

I remember that day, the day my world came crashing down in front of me. I came home thinking everything was fine, but walking in, I realized it was not. It was as though it was in the air; the tide had changed, and walking into the house was beyond heavy that day. Very vividly, I remember my mother-in-law coming over and Dawn talking with her in the kitchen. Her mom said to the boys, "Let's go for a ride and go see what Granddad is doing at the house," and they quickly left.

I didn't know she was coming over. It caught me by surprise, and when I looked at Dawn's face, I could tell something was wrong. She asked me to come into the living room and sit down because she had to talk to me about something. I could feel my stomach start to drop and the anxiety kick in. I was probably the most scared in that moment I have ever been. I knew something wasn't right but couldn't fathom what it was. In my mind, I was thinking back on that day and even days before, trying to figure out what I could have done to make her so upset that the boys needed to go away for us to talk.

I remember the expression on her face when she said those words, "I had an affair." I couldn't believe it because I didn't think it would ever happen to me. I am a very loyal person—probably to a fault—so it was hard to believe that someone I loved and would die for could betray me in such a way. With a friend of mine, at that. I remember over the next couple of days just lying on the bathroom floor crying uncontrollably, with pain I can't even explain going through my body. It was the worst pain and heartache I have ever felt. The emotions I went through are something I will never forget.

The first few weeks after everything came out, I had some pretty rough emotions and feelings, not only toward Dawn but also toward the man involved, who I thought was one of my closest friends at the time. When Dawn came out with everything, it devastated me. I wanted to yell and punch everything, which is nothing like me whatsoever. I was disgusted that anyone could do that to someone else, especially a person who I thought loved me.

I remember waking up crying in the middle of the night out of a deep sleep. If you know me, you know I sleep hard. So this was so deep and painful that I was even going through it in my sleep. Everything was running through my mind 24/7. I would wake up and ask God why this was happening to me and our family. I would wake Dawn up in the middle of the night and ask her why, why, why did she do this to our family. All I could think about was the boys and how this was going to affect them—not only in the short term, but over the long term if our marriage didn't last.

At one point, I had an overwhelming urge to get rid of everything that reminded me of him, the guy who was supposed to be my friend but who I don't think ever truly was. Surprisingly, there was a lot, so I started to purge things because I wanted it all gone. There was music stuff, church things, and for some reason, personal things he was storing at our house. With one thing in particular, his lawnmower, I remember loading it in my car, driving over to his house, and throwing it in the middle of his driveway. My thought was that at some point he would have to leave his house to come out and move it. At that moment, I wanted him to know I was still here and that I could show up at any time. That feeling was strange and relieving all at the same time: strange because it was very unlike me and it was wrong; relieving because at that moment, the pain was so deep I was doing anything and everything to alleviate it.

My feelings of betrayal from the person I thought was my friend hurt badly. I am very trusting, taking people at their word, so I believe that if you say you are going to do something, you will do it. If you say you are going to be there for someone, you are there for them. But with this individual, I believe our friendship was built on a lie from the very beginning.

Those first couple of months were really rough. But I made the decision to forgive Dawn and focus on making our marriage work. I knew a crucial step for us was to go to counseling. We asked for advice on counselors from friends who stuck around and were given a person's name. I called and set up an appointment. We walked in, and immediately something felt off. This was all new to Dawn and me, but it was a referral, so we went with it. The guy was weird right off the bat. We quickly learned that not every counselor is a good one. Not only did we get a weird vibe from this guy, but he put all the blame on me and also insisted on a group hug with him at the end of the session. That was the end of that, and Dawn and I agreed we were going to find someone else.

After that, I researched on my own for new counselors, and God brought us the perfect one. Reading her bio, I knew she was the one, and thankfully she in fact was. The work she put in for both Dawn and me was unparalleled, and I know we wouldn't be where we are today without her help.

Trust is a hard thing to gain back, especially in this situation of betrayal. It was not easy for Dawn to gain my trust back. Counseling helped, and even more, being with each other daily during this time was vital. Even when I didn't want to look at her or be around her, I chose to, because I knew it was important. Spending time praying daily by myself and with each other was also crucial. She also knew staying by my side and walking through this together was the only way we would make it out of this. I honestly needed to know everything, even every dirty detail, to start allowing myself to trust her again. It was excruciating hearing the things that they did and the places they would go to meet and looking back on excuses they would make, things they would say they had to do and then go and meet up. Yet, I wanted to leave no stone unturned, no questions unanswered, and she knew that. I felt that if she could tell me everything that happened—good, bad, and ugly—it would allow me to start trusting and forgiving her. In the end, it was all worth it.

Our marriage today is so much stronger. If we can make it through what we went through, we can get through anything. What a sigh of relief, because a lot of people don't make it through when infidelity is present. I believe God allowed us to go through this to tell our story and share the hope of Jesus with other couples that are going or have gone through this. If we can help one couple make it through, or give them hope that they can make it through, it is all worth it.

The freedom and blessings I have received from God for forgiving both her and the other person are more powerful than words can express. Even more, the freedom to forgive someone, even though an apology was never given, is something that can only be given by the Lord. Unfortunately, I have never received an apology from the man who was one of my closest friends. I point that out not to be petty or critical, but to give understanding that even when you don't get what you think you need or deserve, you still have to be obedient to what scripture calls us to do, and that is to forgive. Christ didn't deserve to die, nor did any of us deserve His forgiveness. Yet, He still did, and we still received.

It is only through Jesus Christ that I was able to forgive. Being able to forgive a person and/or persons who betrayed my trust and love for them was something that it took a while to truly and wholly do, even for me. For something that normally comes easy for me, it didn't this time. Yet I did it through the strength of my God because it is what I am commanded to do in scripture.

It is very important to forgive in order to move forward with your life and not let anger, sadness, and bitterness take control. It would have been very easy to give in to those feelings of hurt and anger and use them as an excuse or as leverage. But that would mean keeping myself in chains and not living in the freedom of the cross. I choose not to live like that. I know forgiveness doesn't come easy for many, so I pray that if it's not easy for you to forgive, God will give you peace about it and the power to do it. Remember that Jesus died on the cross for you and forgave your sins, so in return, we have to forgive others no matter the situation. Our situation was just about as bad as it could get. Yet I chose forgiveness. And because I chose that, Dawn and I are mended. I love her with my whole heart. I trust her completely, and I know that the Lord is using us for Him. This is the result of obedience and living out the gospel.

Thinking back on who and how Dawn was when we first met and married to now: Man, what a difference! The insecure Dawn is now the confident Dawn. She is all in on sharing the gospel and sharing our story with anyone who needs to hear it. She is not afraid to stand up and speak out. She blows me away every time I see her stand up on a stage and speak, sharing the gospel. She has an amazing testimony, and I love watching all God has in store for her and our family. I am all in on this ride and all in on my beautiful bride.

Many ask me the question "How do I forgive someone for _____" (fill in the blank). The answer is the same way I forgave Dawn. I looked her in the eyes and said, "I have a God who forgave me for my sins, how dare I not forgive you."

Living in unforgiveness toward someone is living in disobedience to the gospel. It is our duty as believers to forgive others just as He forgave us. No matter what. What Jesus did for you, He did for them. And there is freedom in forgiveness towards others. The burden borne when holding onto bitterness, anger, and unforgiveness is a burden too heavy to bear. It will eat you up from the inside out; it will distort the heart healing that only comes through the love of a Savior, and it can and will debilitate your relationship with Him.

None of this happens without surrender. Yielding to the instruction and guidance of our God goes against the grain of this broken world. Yet, at the same time, it is the most freeing and life-sustaining thing you could ever do.

I chose to love Dawn, even still.

Chapter Five

The Inner Circle

The doorbell wouldn't stop ringing. I sat frozen at the kitchen table, wondering why whoever it was would not go away. Just when I thought they were gone, it would ring again. It had been two weeks since the news had spread. I had not ventured out much for fear I'd run into someone. The only place I had attempted to go was the grocery store, and even there I saw an acquaintance who did a quick about-face in the aisle to avoid me. A woman who had always said hello to me in the halls of the church now wouldn't even pass me in the grocery store. Why would someone be at my doorstep right now, and obviously not leaving?

With the clear notion that they were not going anywhere, I finally crept up to the front window to peek out. I caught a glimpse of her hair and knew immediately who it was. A friend whose beautiful locks I had always been envious of was standing unmoved, waiting for me to open the door. She was someone from church whom I had known for years.

She was a bold, determined woman who had also seen some brokenness in her own life, so I knew she would not leave until I opened that door. So finally, I did.

Nothing was said; we simply looked at each other, and then she quickly embraced me in a hug as I melted into a puddle of tears. Right there in my foyer, we stood for what seemed like hours, her hugging me tight and me sobbing. Those loud gasps and endless tears felt like a huge release. It was a release, a relief, that I still had a friend. A relief that she was able to see past the pain and betrayal and comfort me. A relief that she loved me despite all I'd done.

At this point, I didn't know who was left who even wanted to be my friend, and I was scared to find out. One of the thoughts I had as my doorbell rang was that it was someone who just wanted to tell me what a horrible human being I was. This was a regular recurring thought in my mind as of late. So the fact that she pursued me at that moment simply to comfort me was another glimpse of grace shown in the midst of mass chaos. I knew I didn't deserve comforting from a friend right then, but it still came.

This is how the Lord can work in these moments. Even in our biggest blunders, He is working for His glory and our good. It is something so hard to wrap our minds around because it just doesn't seem right. Oh, but Jesus, what a glorious Savior.

Those Who Stayed the Course: The Inner Circle

Not only was I scared to open my door when the doorbell rang, but I was also scared to open my email on the daily. I didn't know what I would find each time I clicked that little envelope. But this particular day, a few weeks later, was a sweet one. While I was still in the depths of shame and sorrow over what I had done and all the people I had hurt, mostly secluding myself from everyone and everything, this special note arrived in my inbox. Remember the woman I spoke of in Chapter Two who stopped the rumor mill? She had now sent me an email. The subject line simply said, "Sending some LOVE." That subject in and of itself was a solace. This sweet lady, who, at that time, I did not know very well, wrote, "I just wanted to send you some love and let you know I'm thinking of you. You and your sweet family are in my prayers, day and night."

Tears came, relief was felt, and Jesus was revealed through someone else. I still have this email today because it was a marked moment of healing. Years later, she would share with me that in those dark days she was deeply burdened for me, and the Lord had told her to send that email. She needed to be a beacon of compassion to me. She is now in my inner circle, one of the most trusted friends I have today.

Another friend would randomly call me at 10:07 p.m. and tell me she was picking me up for a late-night run to Walmart (only because Target was closed), knowing that I wasn't going to find sleep any time soon. She just wanted to help give my mind a break because she knew the silence at night could be deafening. The entire way, worship music would blare from the stereo, both of us singing at the top of our lungs, while weary tears would sneak down my face. My dear friend would pretend she had some shopping to do, but both of us knew she just needed to rescue me in those moments. She is part of that inner circle.

Another sweet group of friends bloomed from this brokenness like nothing I'd ever seen. It is my Chicks 'n' Hens. These are six women who were friends of mine, but most were not friends with each other. They range in age from thirty-something to seventy-something, have big personalities, and are lovers of Jesus who make for the wildest bunch you ever did see. To this day, we have a blast together, laugh together, cry together, speak *truth* to each other, and pray for one another. It is beautiful in its own way. I don't believe that, had I not journeyed through what I had, it would have culminated the way it did: in a circle within the inner circle.

The church had become a scary place for me because various spaces throughout the building held a lot of hard and haunting memories. Jeremy and I had prayed for hours upon hours over if we needed to leave our church and start anew. We sought counsel over it, we wrestled with it, we talked it through over and over, and I even consulted several in my inner circle. This was a church I had been on staff at, a church our children had grown up in and a place of people who were very much a family to us. We wept over this, ached over this, and in the end felt the Lord saying, "Stay." Yet at the same time, I could not bring myself to set foot in there. Even driving by it brought a pain to my heart that cut deep into the corners that had not yet been reconciled.

This was one of the consequences of my sin that cut deeply. But the time had come when we needed to be back in the fellowship of church. It was imperative to be sitting in worship, letting truth pour over us, being in community. Many said things so visceral and vile about us not leaving, that it not only hurt me, it hurt my husband deeply. Yet as strange and wrong as many people thought it was, God didn't move us from that particular church.

In the middle of that hard decision, the most priceless story of those awful early days took place, and it is a story engraved on my soul forever. It was the most extraordinary, stamped-in-my-memory, fundamental moment of friendship from those initial days of brokenness, an encounter with one of the wisest women I know, who is also one of my most cherished friends and mentors to this day. It was the most tender yet intense moment I had in that sacred circle. It was a practical tool that turned into a transformative experience where the Holy Spirit was working overtime. Is that even a thing, overtime for the Holy Spirit?

The week before we planned to go back to church, I was sitting at lunch with this friend, sharing with her how terrified I was of entering that building. It was a sad state to be in, a pitiful point when your place of worship, a place so holy to the heart of our God, has become scary. It was scary because sin had made its home in that place. It had been perverted, breaching the hallowed walls, and the enemy was flooding my mind with memories, trying to defeat me. His one objective here was to devastate my mind to the point where I was so worn out that I had no desire to go back.

Thankfully, this dear member of my inner circle happened to be on our church staff. So, that Saturday, late into the evening when we knew no one would be at the church building, she took me there. Just she and I quietly entered, walking the halls and breaching the spaces that had to once again become pure to me. As I walked in, the stillness was loud. I could feel my heart beating faster and faster, and my guilt building higher and higher. With each step I took, more memories flooded in. To my right was the corner where he looked at me when no one else saw and smiled that smile. To my left was the place where we would whisper to each other quickly before anyone spotted us. A little further in, a little deeper into the memories.

I had to remember to breathe as I wept. My knees were weak and my heart was grieved. We were turning the corners of calloused places, entering the rooms of secret exchanges, standing on holy ground that had been hollowed out by sin. As we walked, she prayed. As we entered those ruined spaces, she spoke truth over me. She held my hand as I cried and let God's Word wash over me. She hugged my body as it trembled from the cries that surged from my soul as memories and heartbreak ravaged my being.

This was a moment I will never forget, another marked moment in the healing. The Holy Spirit was ever-present while the enemy was evicted. I believe that at that very moment, a war was raging over my soul. The battle ensued over who would take victory in my life. As I cried, my friend spoke the truth, and the enemy had no place. The enemy left that night. He left my being, and he left that church building. The Lord restored afresh that space for me. The memories and the pain washed away in that moment. It was done and gone because a friend, an inner circle confidant, chose to stay the course, do the hard things beside me, and fight for the life of my soul.

Moments like these are not for the faint of heart. They could not happen as this one did without the help of the ultimate Healer who worked in a mighty way through that dear friend. That night was a transformative night for me. It was one of the bigger steps in this painful, gut-wrenching process. I believe that in that time together, that sweet sister in Christ was clinging to the Savior just as much as I was. As that encounter happened, I was confident that the Savior of the world was gazing down at us, basking in the glow of His glory, knowing what a monumental moment this was going to be. There might have been a special hue of light beaming from that building that night, a blaze of glory glowing all the way to heaven. Who knows? It was a night that took place only because of an obedient step from a wise and faithful friend, despite my very unfaithful moments.

The inner circle is a sacred space for the broken. It is a necessary space, a safe place that only a few are welcomed into. It is a small circle reserved for the ones who will carry the broken to the finish line, to the victory of redemption in Jesus. Through the mud, through the pain, through their own sadness and heartbreak in the situation, they are the true champions in the life of the betrayer. No, it doesn't make sense, those who were hurt and betrayed being part of the rescue for the one who hurt them. Yet it is in the perplexity of these things that we see God's glory shine the most.

The gratitude I have for those who did indeed stay the course is inexpressible because it is imperative to walk with the wise so that you in turn are wise. In my months of brokenness, sorrow, and despair, I had no other choice but to surround myself with wise truth-speakers. "The one who walks with the wise will become wise, but a companion of fools will suffer harm" (Proverbs 13:20). As Frank Gaebelein's 2013 Bible commentary adds, "Proper company contributes to safety and growth." I have no doubt that the safety and growth of my heart were dependent on whom I chose to seek help from. My soul was at stake. If I had chosen any other way, I am confident my rescue mission would have simply been a recovery mission for a body. That may seem a little dramatic, but I can assure you, it is the truth.

My inner circle of women are ladies who will be in my life forever. They are women who met me in the ugliest spaces I have ever been in, and they didn't run. Instead, they jumped into the fire with me, most feeling a little bit of the burn themselves. Yet they kept limping alongside of me to the finish line. They gave of their time, which was time away from their own families. They provided a listening ear for hard and painful things, bathed me in prayer, and spoke God's Word into my life over and over again, never ceasing to offer an encouraging word. They turned me around when I wanted to run away and give up, instead pointing me back to Jesus at every crossroads.

It was also beautiful to see those who stood by and encouraged Jeremy. It is a different space for men to be able to surround one another when the emotions are big and their friend is weeping. He had one friend in particular who loved him so well, held him as he cried, and checked on him practically daily. He never pushed his *opinions* on Jeremy, holding space for Jeremy to grieve and make his own choices while speaking truth over him, encouraging him, and being a rescue when he needed it. He held to the belief that Jeremy was navigating this with the Lord and doing what God had called him to do, and didn't judge Jeremy for the choices he made. He simply loved even still, no matter what.

I do think it is important to acknowledge here that sometimes the inner circle won't show up like ours did. It might be that the silence from your friends is beyond deafening and never-ending. Maybe the storm that hit took out every person you called a friend. Can I fill this space with the cliché yet very true statement that Jesus is a friend to the friendless? In that space where you feel alone, He is truly still there. He knows you better than you know yourself, and He sees your heart clearer than you ever will. So even in the aftermath, the shrapnel, remember that no matter what, He stands holding you up, giving you breath in your lungs and hope in your soul. While you wait for Him to send that earthly friend your way, trust your whole self with Him solely.

Those Who Did Not Stay

When my life was shattered into a thousand pieces, that included friend-ships. Friends were hurt and angry; the betrayal completely broke the bonds of numerous relationships, rendering them unsalvageable. There were several friends caught right in the middle of the mess—a mess they didn't choose, but it pierced them anyway. There were people Jeremy and I cared deeply for, and I do believe they cared deeply for us. This mess was just too much to bear.

It is said that oftentimes there are people who are only in your lives for a season. I think that is true, and some friendships may only be for a time. Sometimes those friendships end abruptly because friends are forced out by circumstance. Many walked away from us, leaving the dumpster fire I created burning in their wake, and never looked back. These relationships died a brutal death, and nothing would revive them. Some of these were friends I'd had for most of my life, and to this day, the memory of losing them leaks a bit of pain into my heart.

One of the problems with mass explosions of sin that leave shrapnel everywhere is the chaos of untruths, gossip, and assumptions spoken in your friends' ears. This can pierce what you think is impenetrable, the deepest of relationships, setting them ablaze. It's an inferno, dangerous flames of turmoil and disorder sweeping through the souls of many, and all that is left when the fire subsides is the ashes of friendship, pieces that can't be glued back together.

It was devastating but understandable. How does one distinguish between truth and lies when there is so much to untangle? How can someone be faulted for washing their hands of everything about you when all they're looking at right now is a liar and a cheat? When everyone around them is shouting, "Run away," "She's not worth it," "She's a fraud" and imparting their own "truths," it would take a miracle for anyone to choose to give somebody a chance.

There isn't much more to say about those who ran. I wish it could have been different, but it wasn't. It wasn't mine to choose, but it was a casualty of my choices.

It was painful to lose them, but it was most excruciating to watch my husband lose some of his friends because of my choices. It is a hard thing for onlookers to have an opinion as to how things should be handled, and when someone handles it differently, some find it even harder to stick around. Many thought Jeremy went too easy on me or should have walked away; they couldn't understand his actions, which in turn resulted in the breaking of friendships.

To this day, it is one of my deepest prayers that the Lord will give me a chance to sit with these people again. It would be simply for Him to receive the glory in reconciliation—not so we could recover our friendships necessarily, but just so we could once more be sisters and brothers in Him. That day will probably not happen until we meet in glory, but it will never cease being one of my prayers in my time with the Lord each day, because who knows? We serve a mighty God, and maybe He will open that door on this side of eternity. If He does, all glory to Him, and what a beautiful day it will be. If He doesn't, all glory to Him, and it is simply one more thing I look forward to in eternity.

In Conclusion

I believe God goes before and prepares the hearts of each and every individual who is impacted by these awful situations. Losing friendships is part of that ripple effect of sin. Yet, when sin implodes, it does not take our God by surprise. I imagine Him sitting up in the heavens, His heart aching with sadness as He watches the devastation hit. At the same time, there is a wave of peace because He knows He has already prepared the hearts and minds of those entangled. He sees the victory and glory that will come in the end.

Jesus gives a beautiful illustration of this, as He always remains trustworthy in all of our untrusted moments. What a beautiful thing it is when we can represent Jesus in this way and be a trusted confidant to someone who has been untrustworthy with us. That, my friend, is love lived out. That is the gospel illustrated in a way that draws an awed gaze from those on the outside looking in. And for the soul being ministered to—me in this story—it is an aspect of love that penetrates parts of a heart that have been dark for a long time. To see these friends rise to the challenge and stay the course with me was life-changing. I never expected the love and compassion I received, and I most certainly didn't deserve it. Yet there it was, through God's people. It opened the door for me to be filled with the wisdom of God's Word, and to become the person I am today.

In Exodus 17, there is a story about Moses winning a battle, but only when his arms are raised in the air with the staff of God in his hand. He becomes tired and cannot keep his arms in the air. Aaron and Hur are with him and realize what is happening. They come alongside Moses, putting a stone under him so that he can sit, and then they each raise one of Moses' arms so that the war can be won. Isn't this just a beautiful picture of community?

It should be the same for us, and it most certainly was for me. Whatever battle is raging in our lives, it is an overwhelming symphony of God's grace when we can come alongside our fellow brothers and sisters in Christ and raise one of their arms to help the battle be won. This raising of arms could mean interceding on their behalf in prayer, or it could be more practical things such as a hot meal or an encouraging word. It could also be physically picking them up off the floor when they can't do it themselves. It could be speaking life into the frailty of their current circumstances. It could be helping them pick up the pieces and encouraging them to take that next step forward.

There are so many miraculous ways we can "raise the arms" of our weary friends. The many friends who carried my arms held high to our good God for months on end are the very reason I made it out alive—and not only alive, but made new, fully transformed, and whole.

There is no handbook on how to walk out of these situations. There is no particular step-by-step method that will work every time. The only tried and true resources to take hold of are the guidance of God's Word and the wisdom of the Holy Spirit relayed through it. Even with that, the way He leads each individual in each situation will be different. As friends, the church body, and onlookers, we must understand this and not judge, criticize, or "would have/should have" someone. What you *think* you'd do in a certain situation changes when you actually find yourself in the situation.

I believe there is a caveat that should be stated in all of this. Please understand that I am not encouraging people to put themselves in harm's way to be hurt repeatedly. Let me be clear in stating that continuing a relationship with someone who has broken trust should only happen when there is clear evidence of repentance and brokenness, and that someone is moving towards growth and transformation. This chapter, or rather this entire book, is in no way implying that anyone should stay in a toxic environment where change isn't evident.

In the years since, I have had many conversations with people who were on the periphery of my story: those who were on the sideline, watching in the wings, maybe people you would call "friends but not friends." Do you know what I mean? One of the biggest takeaways from these conversations that I heard over and over was "I just didn't know what to say," or "I just didn't know what to do."

It makes complete sense. When situations like this happen, it is hard to know what to say. It is this odd dichotomy where you might be thinking, "What they did was horrible!" Yet, at the same time, you are saddened by the choices they made and the impact they are having on everything and everyone around them now. You want to reach out because you feel like the Lord is asking you to, but you aren't sure what words are right because "I'm sorry" just doesn't seem to fit. Here are a few tips:

Just send a text that says something like "You don't need to respond, I just want you to know that you are thought of and prayed for." Something so simple can be the lifeline needed at that very moment.

Send a card. Call me old-fashioned, but I still get giddy when receiving a physical card in the mail. The card doesn't have to say a lot. Just a simple encouragement is all that is needed.

No matter what you do or how you send it, someone in a situation of coping with the depravity and consequences of their sin just needs to know a few key things:

- That they aren't alone

- That someone still cares

- That God isn't finished yet

- To just keep going

Don't pry. Don't do it just to be on this side of the gossip. Do it because you are grieved for them and want to extend the compassion of our God. If your intentions aren't pure, don't do it. If you are doing it with the Lord's leading, it is a beautiful thing, because a loyal friend in disloyal moments is Jesus exemplified.

Chapter Six

A Place of Grace

There we sat in our pastor's office, Jeremy and I on one side of the desk, our pastor on the other, the day after it all came out. This went down as one of the more humiliating moments I experienced: sitting there, being asked some of the most awkward and painful questions by our pastor and friend, and answering them with my husband right next to me. I wanted to run far and fast to get out of this. "Were there physical boundaries crossed?" I tried not to answer, hesitating, only half answering, but he wasn't buying it. Pushing me, challenging me. It was a position I had put myself in that was unimaginable. I knew the only way to get through it was just to be more and more forthcoming.

As I did that, Jeremy sat there wailing, a sound I had never heard escape my husband's body, and one I never wanted to hear again. Unable to watch him weeping to my left, I kept looking forward into the face of our pastor and his response to me, another expression I wished I'd never had to see. Betrayal, lies, heartbreak, and grief were all brimming up to the surface. The light was on, the secrets exposed, and everything was broken.

I left that day knowing I was doomed. I had now completely devastated my husband, lost my job, and broken trust seemingly beyond repair all around me. As Jeremy was grappling with it all on the drive home, he called one of his closest friends sobbing, saying over and over, "Dawn has broken my heart, Dawn has broken my heart."

What does one do in that moment? I didn't have a clue. I just kept staring straight ahead, driving, because he was so distraught, he couldn't even drive. All I could think was that I was the worst person on planet Earth, I was losing it all, and there was no coming back from this. Everything was destroyed. Never did I think, and especially not right then and there, that along with my husband, the staff and church community as a whole would rally around us, and extend immeasurable grace and love. I was convinced we would never walk into the doors of that church again. I had resolved that we, if there was even going to be a we, would have to find a new place to attend church. Even worse, our children would have to start all over finding new friends in a new place of worship, all because of me. I was confident there was no way I would ever work in ministry again, most certainly not at the same church. It was the end.

In these situations, the normal response of the church world is one of two things. The first is rushing the restoration process to quickly get back to business like nothing ever happened. In this scenario, the broken people are forgotten in the process, most often not healing properly. The second response is simply putting it on the shelf, leaving both parties of the offense in question to depart, figure it out themselves, and allow the church to move on without them.

By the grace of God, our church did neither of those things, exemplifying the restoration process in one of the most incredible ways I have ever seen. While there was anger and hurt and deep heartache over what happened, everyone from our pastor to my dear friends on staff to others in leadership landed on the fact that this was a deep-rooted sin and we needed help, not abandonment. They took themselves out of the equation, surrendering their own pain to the healing balm of Jesus, and set out to carry us through. It wasn't easy, it wasn't perfect, and hiccups did arise. However, it was a Spirit-led process that the Lord worked through miraculously. What a privilege and blessing it was to be the recipient of this. I often wonder why God chose me to be the beneficiary of such an offering.

Despite the devastation of that first day of confessions and pain, the church stepped in and lined up counseling for us and had several people do practical things like bring food to us. Others willingly took our boys to the children's activities so they didn't miss a beat. It was an immediate outpouring of compassion and a living and active expression of grace.

Word began to spread, rumors were born, and stories began to take on lives of their own. When you are in a large public arena such as this, it is inevitable. Yet, over and over we saw the staff and leadership take the lead in shutting down gossip, pointing to Jesus, and continually encouraging us while strongly holding me accountable. It was a delicate balance of all the things, carefully treaded only through the wisdom of the Holy Spirit. It was a tall task, and I know it was painful, yet they all stood in the trenches taking punches for something I caused. Talk about grace upon grace.

For the first few months, we were floundering, trying to take steps forward in healing and basic survival. So, while we were being ministered to by the church, we weren't attending church at the time. While I continued to pray about it, I had left the decision of staying or leaving our church in Jeremy's hands. I didn't know what the answer was and actually wanted him to be able to decide more than anything. I was simply trying to stay upright and fight for my marriage, my integrity, and my character. I didn't think I deserved to choose.

A few months in, Jeremy came to me and said, "I don't think we need to leave. I want to stay." While panic set in on the inside, I simply said, "Okay." I couldn't imagine walking the halls again, the stares I would get, the whispers I would hear. I envisioned walking in with a giant red "A" on my shirt every single Sunday. I might as well just get a banner saying "The harlot is here!" Yet I wanted to do whatever Jeremy felt was right, and in addition, the Lord had told me the same thing, even though I didn't want to acknowledge it.

In the week leading up to our return, major panic set in within my soul. I had no idea what to expect, wondering who would say hello and who would shun me. Some might come up and punch me for all I knew. My mind was going everywhere, mostly in the worst possible direction, and I was terrified.

While the leadership was understandably nervous and apprehensive, we had their support to come back. To avoid distractions and unnecessary encounters, they told us they would walk us quietly into worship to sit and help us leave the same way. It still wasn't making me feel better. Yet I knew we needed to be there. It was important to be sitting and soaking in truth with the community.

Many thought, and you might be thinking too, "Why don't you just go somewhere else? There are churches on every corner." Not to worry, I thought the same thing. Something kept pulling us back, drawing us to stay. *It was home.* At the time, most of the decisions we made were for our children's sake. At ten years old, they didn't know what was happening, and we didn't want to disrupt their safety net of people they had known for their entire lives. At the same time, it sure did seem easier to just run away and go somewhere else; the kids would be just fine. All true, but again, it was as though there was a hard stop every time we looked at going somewhere else. At this moment, we were choosing the really hard route of staying, but sometimes that is what God asks us to do. I would dare to say, most times that is what God asks us to do—choose the hard. Growth comes most deeply through walking out the hard, instead of running to the easy.

The first Sunday morning we chose to go was very hard. Jeremy grabbed my hand and we walked in, together, a team ready to do battle. To this day, I am unsure if friends were strategically placed throughout to catch us or if the King of the Universe simply did it. But, from the front door to the worship center, there they were. One sweet friend was standing just inside the doors to embrace us with a hug as soon as we walked in. As we entered the worship center, two seats were held by another smiling familiar face preserving a safe space for us. There we sat, a few people coming with hugs, encouraging words, and an extra embrace of comfort to let us know they were rooting for us. I believe that first Sunday the Lord blinded both Jeremy and me to any uncomfortable glances, glaring eyes, and kept us from hearing any divisive chatter.

We left just after the service and knew somehow our church family was going to be a champion in this story. Our good God had reassured us that morning through His faithful followers.

Each Sunday it seemed a little bit easier, some more than others. I'd be remiss if I didn't admit that there were some Sundays that were just too much for me. I'd become overwhelmed, and the enemy was relentless in his attacks, trying to take me out once and for all. I seemed too weak to bear it. Sometimes, it was something as simple as needing to slip out of worship because a song sent me spiraling, and I never wanted to disrupt Jeremy's worship. (I'd disrupted enough of his life at this point. . . .) So there was an office, the office of my dear friend, always open and available for me to run to, close the door, and weep. I would escape to this welcomed room, curl up on the couch, and cry out to the Lord to ease the pain. I'd do what I needed to do to get through it. Her inviting, soft, velvety-blue couch enveloped me in all the necessary moments, and somehow she always knew when I was there, because as the couch comforted my body, I'd always hear her words begin to comfort my soul. It was just another way the church stepped up and supported, by having that safe space ready and available.

These things aren't special ways to protect those who have screwed up. Don't get that twisted. These were havens for the broken. These were elements of security in a journey of healing. They were ways to extend the relentless love of our Savior to a broken vessel who was trying to limp her way back. This is the way of our Maker that we should live out, and the church was doing just that.

This didn't stop those who thought letting me back in was wrong. They still made it clear that was their belief. It didn't stop the naysayers. It didn't end the procession of those who walked down the hall past me with a snicker, a smirk, or a look of pure disdain. Questions came constantly, and they came hard. How could you ever trust her again? How do you overcome the questioning and doubt? She's a scandal, she's a disgrace, she brings the drama, and on and on the comments grew.

Criticism always comes with how churches handle many situations, problems, and changes, but with something like this, it comes fast and furious. Our pastor had to combat a lot of critique for letting us stay at the church and also carrying me through the restoration process. His response always came with gently reminding others that we are *all* sinners. It is something that will always remain dear to me, knowing that despite my betrayal, despite the chaos that ensued from my doings, he saw my brokenness, he saw my desire to heal and grow, and he fought for us. They all did, the entire leadership of the church. It is a treasured jewel in my healing story, and watching them do that for me has spurred me to be willing to do that for others. This is, once again, living out the gospel.

Months into this journey, going to church became a little more normal again. Sweet friends in leadership were beginning to welcome me into small tasks: helping with childcare, helping with administrative tasks, and everything in between. I was being welcomed back into a space of behind-the-scenes responsibilities. No one needed to know, it wasn't anyone's business. It was just a small affirmation from those closest to me, saying they saw me, they knew me, and they could see the transformation in my life and my heart taking shape. While being asked to do things in a ministry space wasn't an end goal for me, it was a beautiful confirmation of the Lord doing His work and a reminder that He wasn't done with me.

Leadership at the church saw the changes, heard the reports of goodness, and celebrated those steps with us, all the while holding me accountable. As celebrations happened, serving started. Bringing me back into the fold of serving began in very small steps. I loved being given small, quiet tasks to help, peacefully serving in the background. The beautiful thing was that this kind of serving ministered to my heart in ways I cannot even explain. They were simple kingdom tasks that established giant affirmations in my heart that I was seen, I was loved, and my coworkers knew God was working.

Many months into healing, the leader of women's ministry at the time asked me to be a driver for our upcoming speaker. My response was, oh, that's too much, I probably don't deserve to do that. Her response was, "I want you and only you to be that driver." She ignored my insecurity and affirmed my invitation. That guest speaker was Kay Arthur. I took that precious woman to and from her hotel, and on the second day, as we were driving back to her hotel, she asked me, "Dawn, what's your story?" *Umm . . . that's a loaded question,* I thought. My second thought was that if she found out what I had done just the previous year, she might refuse to ride with me. But somehow I ended up sitting in my car, sharing my story with Kay Arthur. Only Jesus. She sat, listened, wept with me, and then prayed over me. She looked at me, cradled my face in her hands, and said, "Oh, my precious Dawn, I love you, dear. You know our Lord has forgiven you, and you now have to walk in that and live like you believe it!" She went on to quote some beautiful passages of scripture to me and hugged me.

This was yet another marked moment of healing that would not have happened had the precious woman leading women's ministry not taken the leap and let me do that task.

The church also played a big role in protecting our kiddos. Often, children of people in ministry suffer deeply when their parents screw up. They see churches turn their backs on them, they see the awful things said about their parents, and the list goes on. We were counseled early on not to tell our boys what had happened at the time. We were encouraged to shelter them as long as possible. That is no small task in today's world. The bottom line was that they were ten, and a ten-year-old doesn't need to hold the responsibility or pain of such deep turmoil. We chose to listen to this counsel and would encourage anyone in the same shoes as us today to do the same.

There was always a listening ear or protective arms around, making sure no one was talking about it or saying things to our children that they shouldn't be. God did miraculous things through His church to hold that hedge of protection. It wasn't until years later that we began to share with them more of what had happened. I was actually able to use it as a lesson in some challenging days we had with them. It is important to be authentic and honest with our children about our shortcomings, but it is also important to be wise about the timing. Through it all, we were grateful for the church leadership teaming up to help maintain the normalcy of childhood for our boys while we battled for new stability in our marriage.

One of the core values of our church is, "We are a place of grace." This value was lived out exponentially through my story and is another reason why I am who I am today. Those in leadership remained hope-filled for a new beginning. It was about learning lessons through this process and starting afresh; letting the old go, and beginning with a new start. It was always asking the Lord what He would have them learn from this, allowing growth, and building anew upon the lessons learned. They trusted that God was going to do mighty and unique things through this process to reveal Himself and for His glory to be shown. He did just that.

Hope is woven into healing. When the church lives out the hope that is spoken of from the pulpit, healing can come in big ways. Throughout years of healing and restoration, God's glory was revealed in ways undreamt of. Redemption was on the horizon.

Glory in
Redemption

Chapter Seven

Scar Tissue

"I left the church five years ago because of you." Those were the first words that came out of her mouth. "I was angry, bitter, and wanted the worst for you." Expecting something like that but still taken aback, I looked at her and said, "I understand that completely, and I am so sorry." She stopped me right then by putting her hand up. I felt my heartbeat rising, wondering how this was going to end. Was she about to blast me, or punch me? I might have even looked for the closest exit. Then, she proceeded, "That is, until tonight."

That night, five years into my journey, was the night I found myself standing on the very same stage where I had stood, years earlier, leading worship next to the man I was having an affair with. This time, though, I was standing in total freedom, filled with joy like never before, sharing my testimony with over four hundred women. If it sounds terrifying, let me confirm, yes it was. Just before I took the stage, I asked myself what the heck I was doing, thinking I was a glutton for punishment. For a hot second, I believed I didn't have any right to be on that stage and almost got in my car and drove away. That is, until the presence of the Holy Spirit washed over me, and the assurance of a good and merciful Father took hold of my heart. The graciousness of our God whispered to my heart in that moment that this was what He had carried me through it all for. It was now time for me to proclaim *His* greatness, standing boldly before the very people I had betrayed. Standing confidently in front of many in the crowd who had gossiped, gawked, and sneered. It was time. Breathe in, breathe out.

Afterward, the line of people who wanted to hug me, affirm God's work in me, and share their own stories and struggles was long. It was such a beautiful moment. Redemption was in our midst. And yet, through all the encouragement and story-sharing, I kept waiting for the one who would tell me I was a jerk, a harlot, or a scam. It never came. What did come was something I never expected.

She was one of the last ones. I sensed her waiting for a while, and caught her eye a few times between the women who came up. The look on her face was different from everyone else's. I couldn't figure it out and was a bit on edge as she finally approached and began to speak. My inner voice was saying, here it comes, the one who thinks you're a fraud, an imposter, the one who will destroy you with her words. And those first words that escaped her lips, the avowal that she had left the church because of me, confirmed that this was it, she was the one I'd known wanted to unleash her fury on me. Yet, that wasn't what happened.

Instead, she went on to share with me that her friend had told her I was speaking at this event. She admitted she came to hear what I had to say just because she was curious. She expected to sit cynical, snarking at anything that came out of my mouth. Then a smile began to emerge, with a little hesitancy and a hint of apprehension. She went on to apologize to me for harboring such bitterness. That was unexpected! She expressed how listening to my testimony had moved her, and she was confident God had done miraculous things in my life because He was now doing something in her heart. My heart could have leapt out of my chest at that moment as we both began to cry. It was beautiful, God-ordained, mighty kingdom work happening in the here and now. It was one of the moments when I knew the Lord was going to use my story, my mess, for His unrivaled glory.

She didn't have to do that. She didn't have to apologize to me. Truthfully, that sounds so bizarre, because who needs to apologize to the girl who did what I did? That is one of the pearls of redemption in our stories with Jesus, the inconceivable, undeserved things that happen as glorious glimpses of grace. That precious woman could have left that night, and I would have never known. She could have said, "*Well that was nice*," walked out the door, and gone on with her life. However, through her pausing in humility, walking up to me, and sharing all that she did with me, both she and I were changed for the better that night. That is how our God moves and accomplishes His purposes on the redemption road. He brought humility to her heart, and He brought a positive declaration to mine. This exchange declared that God can transform the hardest of hearts, and He will never stop His redeeming work—and most often blows our socks off with how He does it!

His redemption steps heal the deepest, darkest parts of our hearts when we reveal the deepest, most honest parts of our stories. Through these healing strides, He unveils more restorative spaces.

I began to enter the church building with even more ease. That's not to say there weren't still the side-eyes and the whispers. (Heck, that's still happening today.) But I had been instilled with the tools and tactics to withstand it. The most important of those was realizing that it did not matter what others thought and said. What mattered was my right relationship with Jesus. Finally taking hold of that and living it out was one of the most freeing aspects of this walk. Let me tell you that even today, this is one of the most freeing principles in life.

When we live in right relationship with Jesus, aligning our hearts, minds, and souls with Him, everything else falls to the wayside of worry.

As the months and years went on, life continued to move in the right direction. This isn't to say there weren't hard days, because boy, were there! Hard days came in different forms; they could stem from struggles Jeremy was having, challenges I was enduring, or just plain bad days. This is part of the process in any journey, right? Yet we continued to persevere by identifying the problem, asking the Lord for wisdom to move through it (giving us growth in the process), and then tackling it head-on. That is where significant progress happened, on those hard days when we worked through it in wise and healthy ways. (Many lessons from that year of counseling, and specifically surrounding ourselves with wise friends, came into play here.)

During these years of transformation, so much had to happen. Old habits had to be broken, feelings had to dissipate, and memories had to fade. However, time kept moving, healing continued, and restoration was happening: restoration in my heart, in my marriage, in my life, and in the church. Hope was glimmering, sorrow was fading, and newness was on the horizon.

Habits of shame and hiding transformed into victory and joy. Feelings for another person that were completely wrong, inappropriate, and sinful melted away. They were replaced with new and deeper affections for my husband. Memories in various places that once paralyzed me were replaced with new traditions and new routines. These things didn't happen overnight, and they most certainly were not easy. This was months, and in some areas years, of fighting, battling, and overcoming great depths of wreckage. It was not pretty; it was very messy, painful, and had a lot of gut-wrenching phases in it. That is the messiness of sin, the consequences we don't talk about enough. It is the part of the healing process that we will quickly forget when the sin looks inviting. Let this be another reminder to you that whatever it is the evil one is dangling in front of you right now that looks enticing, it is not worth it. It will never be worth it, and in fact, it will momentarily destroy you.

Healing is a messy and long journey. But it is one worth navigating. Restoration is a painful and often excruciating process, but again, so worth it. It is all worth it when we let Jesus in to mend the mess. I never want anyone to think this process is easy or simple from anything I say. Let me be clear in declaring that our stories of healing and redemption will not be fully complete until we are in glory.

I am writing this book ten years later, and there are still some twinges of pain that sneak up. If I told you every day was sunshine and roses, it would be a lie and a discrediting to everything we have walked through. It is important to acknowledge that there are occasions when things will creep up and sting. This is what we call scar tissue.

In our bodies, scar tissue is tissue that forms over a scar where a wound once was. If you have ever had an injury or surgery that led to scar tissue, you may have some tender spots there. When the site of the injury is bumped or rubbed up against, it might give you a little jolt of pain, reminding you of its existence. However, the jolt will usually only last a few seconds, and then it is gone. It gives you a recollection that something was once broken there; even though it is now healed, small reminders will happen.

I believe that in the same way, when we have scars on our soul from a wound that has healed, they can be hit on occasion and give us a jolt of pain. Most times, for me, it is unexpected, but I most definitely rebound quickly.

Here I sit ten years later, and sometimes a song will come on, one that I have heard three thousand times over the last several years. On time 3,001, it gives me a little knock of remembrance that I sang that while leading worship with that man. Eight years ago, that would have taken me out. Today, it gets a little "oh" and then an "eww" and then a "Thank You, Jesus, for redemption."

And I move on.

Those silly Facebook memories that pop up can be brutal. But today, as they pass me by, I breathe easy, say a little prayer of thanksgiving, and move on.

I recently opened up the journal I wrote in just after my world fell apart. It was the first time I had read those words since I'd written them. It took my breath away. I found myself turning the pages with trembling hands. Except the beautiful thing was that even as I felt the pain that I had experienced in those days of heartache and sorrow, in the same breath, I felt the joy and hope that I live in today.

As Jeremy and I recently sat discussing the chapter he so graciously shared with you all, the same thing happened. We were talking about the day I confessed to him. I remarked, "I don't remember much of that day, it was all a blur." He quickly replied, "I remember every single second," as tears welled up in his eyes. I was somewhat taken aback by his reply, and tears welled up in my eyes, too. We sat staring at each other for a moment as if we both felt that pang of memory: his of the pain he endured that day, mine of the pain I inflicted that day. Then, as if someone had snapped their fingers, we started to laugh. We were sitting in a restaurant, and we soon became aware of our surroundings, wondering if people thought we were having a miserable dinner since we both had tears in our eyes. We dabbed our eyes, said "I love you," and enjoyed the rest of our dinner. Scar tissue stings for a moment, but then the healing that has taken place very quickly remedies the temporary discomfort.

All this is to say, don't think that healing on this earth will ever bring you complete wholeness, because it won't. I'd be doing you a disservice if I claimed it did. We live in a broken world, and we will never ever be completely healed until we are in heaven with our Savior. Part of healing is the hope we have that we will one day be with Him, with total healing, in eternity. So whenever you find yourself on the journey of mending a mess, let yourself feel that momentary pain, that scar tissue twinge, and let it be a radiant reminder of all He has done.

As time goes on and healing continues, life is made new, and you begin to hear the echoes of redemption.

Chapter Eight

The Secret Society of Sinners

Friend, if you are in the thick of it right now, scared out of your mind and knowing you are looking down the barrel of a long, hard fight to get your life back, sound the alarm and get out! Stopping and surrendering right now is worth it. Where you took that left turn on the exit ramp to ruin, take a hard right into the arms of our Savior for redemption. It will always be worth it, and the great Creator, Redeemer, and Healer is right here, right now, waiting to mend whatever is broken, healing you. He is ready to do the work with you. The freedom on the other side of that work is so worth it. I am cheering you on, praying for you, and telling you with great passion that our God is with you in it all. I can assure you that He will never leave you in the midst of the mess. He will always fight for you, and He is forever faithful. Do it: Let go of whatever it is right this minute, confess it to the Lord, surrender it at His feet, and begin.

As I walked in on the first Sunday I came back to church, several people came up and hugged me, gave me a little pat on the back, and whispered, "We have been there, you will be okay." When I say it happened repeatedly, I mean it happened countless times. I was stunned at the number of people who, once they knew I was "in the club," felt they could share with me very quietly that they had been there too. While it was nice to know I wasn't alone, I found myself getting a little frustrated and bothered with each whisper that came. It was bizarre.

I had spent weeks upon weeks thinking I was alone in this. Over and over, I would tell myself that no one had ever done anything like this. What I had done, no one could relate to. Yes, people have affairs all the time, it is a sad reality but a true one. However, amidst the fallout, sitting in isolation, my perception was that my affair was the worst ever. I was in the pit, trying to find my way out, hit hard with judgment from the masses and mostly from myself. I had thoroughly convinced myself that no one was as evil as I was.

Where am I going with this? Great question!

Our goal as Christians isn't to be perceived as perfect. Our goal as believers should be to accept that we are hopeless sinners without a Savior, and He can do miraculous works through our major messes. Perfect Patties don't convey the gospel, Broken Betties do. I am not saying we all need to write books on our deepest, darkest secrets; you can leave that to me. I am definitely not saying to go blast your business all over social media. What I am saying is that we do each other a great disservice when we live like we always have it together or like we never screw up. When we only whisper to the ones we know have been there before, but dare not tell anyone else, that causes more damage than you think.

We have to be willing to be vulnerable, share our testimony of God's faithfulness, and exclaim His greatness, despite our weaknesses. And maybe, just maybe, we should even share some of those weaknesses. Maybe, just maybe, we can be willing to share with our small group how we just unloaded our wrath on our children before pulling into the church parking lot. We are able to do this when we feel safe asking this small group to pray for us, because we are confident it won't leave the room or cause judgment. You might even get tips on healthy and encouraging ways to fix it with your children when you leave.

Maybe, in the safe space of our church community, we can share without fear of judgment how our marriage is falling apart, we don't know what the next step is, and we need help. That way, we can first be prayed for and lifted up with truth, but also, our transparency helps the woman sitting next to us who is struggling with the very same thing not to feel alone. Then, in turn, she can feel the safety of sharing too, and then we can all go to the Lord together to pray for miracles. What a beautiful circle of shelter and goodness that could be, happening amongst our fellow believers.

Could we even go a step further and be willing to share in that small safe space our struggle with pornography or lust, or our battle with spending habits, or whatever it is that is swallowing us alive while we sit and silently suffer in shame?

Maybe instead of a secret society of sinners, we can be a saving society of sinners. If we were willing to live in authenticity, this wouldn't be an exclusive club, it would be a "come one, come all" club! It could be a revival. It could see life-changing, transformative magnificence that would draw people in instead of kicking them out. It could see the ashamed come in and ask for help, the pride-filled come in seeking humility, and the shattered come in seeking a reprieve.

We have to start by looking at ourselves and understanding ourselves as sinners in need of a Savior. This begins when we realize the enormity of sin, its damaging effects, and its life-altering results. It starts when we recognize that we are no better than our neighbors, we are just as broken and sinners all the same.

As a whole, I think we often minimize sin. We want to diminish the degree of it. However, at its core, *all* sin is evil, and our God grieves it no matter what it is. From the little white lies on the surface to the depths of destroying your life with deep-rooted deceit, it is all the same evil. It is when we become complacent with the—in our minds—small things that the big things become easy. Never in a million years did I believe I would choose to have an affair—and with my best friend's husband at that. Never did I think I would create some of the most despicable lies one could ever come up with. It all started with one decision that just didn't seem like that big of a deal.

We must all first realize that we are *one* decision away from turning our worlds upside down. We must never be of the mindset that *I would never do that.* That was me. That was me as I looked down on others around me who fell into the unfathomable trap the enemy had laid for them. I surmised that these people were beneath me, that they were weak, terrible people for choosing the bad things that I would never do. Well, that was bad decision number one for me! I am sure you are familiar with the saying, "Pride comes before the fall." It's also found in Proverbs 16:18: "Pride comes before destruction and an arrogant spirit before a fall." When we see ourselves as invulnerable to the traps of the enemy, we will quickly fall prey to his schemes.

The second we see ourselves as above the enemy's games, we are in trouble. The moment we see others' mistakes as things we would never do, our souls are already on their way to being sold to Satan. "Strong words," you might say. I speak from experience.

When we minimize the magnitude of sin, we maximize its ability to access our souls. It is necessary to recognize that sin is an attack on the throne of our hearts, souls, and minds. Our God's rightful place is head over it all; anything less than that is a sin. Anything we choose to fill His place is a sin, no matter how small or inconsequential it seems to us.

Diminishing the awfulness of sin disables our ability to take hold of and treasure the grace that our Savior gives us in His rescuing mercy.

My big misstep began with several small decisions, which I justified all the while. That one small decision to take a secret phone call too late into the night that no one knew about: I minimized it, assuring myself that it was no big deal. I didn't shut down lengthy, inappropriate text conversations either. Instead, I minimized it again: No big deal. The common phrases of justification begin with "No one knows," "It won't lead to anything," and "It's meaningless." Small missteps in justification lead to big errors in judgment.

When we lack accountability in our own lives, and true authenticity within our communities of believers, we will most often not be challenged to bear our burdens or missteps to each other. If we have nowhere to share these deep issues, they will fester, take root, and eventually explode.

The other facet in this equation is that Christians who are part of this secret society of sinners are often the biggest offenders when it comes to spreading gossip or laying down judgment. Ouch. They are the first to turn up a nose or furrow a brow. They are very much like the Pharisees. This sounds like a harsh judgment on my part, I know. But let me be the first to raise my hand and say, hi, it's me, I was the problem.

I say this not to be brutal or critical. I say it from a heart desperate to see change. Desperate to see Christians begin to rally around each other with the supernatural grace and mercy we have all been given and pour it out to others. This kind of living lends itself well to the motto that you give the grace that you require. I have a sweatshirt with that quote, and it's a good reminder.

Over the last several years in ministry, I have watched the reactions of many when they find out the latest rumor about someone else in their Bible study or the girl down the street. I have seen the gossip presented as pretty, little, bow-topped prayer requests, not sincere heartbreak. People only speak of it in this context to have the opportunity to be the first one to break the news, the one *in the know*. It is disgusting.

I've sat with countless women who were broken over the way they were talked about and treated after their lives were exposed in one way or another. Sadly, the Christian culture tends to foster running and distancing ourselves from the one with the most recent plague, while chatting about it with those around us who seem to be above it all too—heavy on the "seem." The prevailing attitude is that being associated with these people would be detrimental to our reputations. Hard stop.

If we stopped and really dove into the scriptures we claim to live by, we would see that Jesus was the very opposite of this. He walked with sinners, ate with them, and broke cultural barriers to reach them. Don't hear what I'm not saying. I am not saying Jesus was okay with someone's sin or affirmed a sinful lifestyle. What I am saying is that He looked past outward actions and appearances to grow a deeper relationship and pour out His love in order to change lives.

Speaking of scripture, one of my favorite accounts in all of God's Word is that of the Samaritan woman, the woman at the well. You can find this in John 4. But Jesus also reached out to so many others in spite of the circumstances: Mary Magdalene who was demon-possessed; the woman with the alabaster jar, known as a sinful woman, in Luke 7; and the woman caught in adultery in John 8, who was publicly shamed but found forgiveness and newness with Jesus. The list goes on.

Jesus didn't sin by breaking down barriers, looking past the outward assumptions and appearances of these people. In the same way, we don't sin by ministering to, encouraging, and speaking to, not *about*, those who are struggling. It is the opposite. When we choose to speak about someone, distance ourselves from someone, or frown upon someone, that is the sin, my friend! When we choose to step out, living out the love of the gospel, we can be a part of the transformative, miraculous work of Jesus! We should care more about the souls of our sisters and brothers than our standing in the "who's who" of the late-breaking gossip. Don't be a blabbermouth; be the representation of the gospel extending grace to the broken. Look more like the Jesus you claim to follow.

It is a hard thing to say, and one I hesitated to say for a long time, but a few of the people who extended me the most grace were those who didn't follow Jesus, and the harshest of my critics were some of the perceived most faithful followers of Him. Something was fishy; it didn't add up. Then, as I observed this, I realized I was one of those critical jerks before I jumped in my own pile of manure. I was the harshly judging "Christian" who ran far away from the one plagued by sin while contributing to the rumor mill. Yep, I am admitting it. My name is Dawn, and I was one of the biggest offenders in this area, a critic and a gossip. So this chapter is preaching to my very own heart and soul.

Do you know why I did that? I had so many insecurities in myself that I wanted to make sure no one was looking back at me, so it was easy to point out all the flaws in someone else's life! I hadn't allowed God to invade all the junk spaces in my own heart, which left me a very critical, gossipy gal. I myself had hurt a lot of people with my hateful, harsh opinions.

Oh, how the tables turned . . .

Never again will you see me pile on the judgment train like it's a conga line, and dance all over someone else's blunder while ignoring my own. And I pray that, after reading this, you might think twice about doing it yourself.

When we point the finger at someone else, it is imperative that we remember the four fingers still pointing back at us. Have you heard that before? Probably. Take hold of it, because it's true. Your secret sin is no less real than the loud one being exposed right now. Did you hear the mic drop?

So, let's take this secret society of sinners and change the world. Drop the facades, the criticisms, and the gossip, and live out love—*agape* love.

Galatians 6:2–5 says, "Carry one another's burdens; in this way you will fulfill the law of Christ. For if anyone considers himself to be something when he is nothing, he is deceiving himself. But each person should examine his own work, and then he will have a reason for boasting in himself alone, and not in respect to someone else. For each person will have to carry his own load."

Those faithful friends who disregarded the gossip, didn't believe the outrageous stories spoken of me, and ignored the appeals to abandon me are those I will hold dear to my heart until the day I die. They are the ones who lived like Jesus: They looked past the flaws and missteps and were willing to get in the trenches with me. These friends are one of the reasons I am who I am today. Jesus used them in extraordinary ways.

Because of this, I challenge you today to be that for someone else. Be that for someone who is facing a hard time or just imploded their life. Don't listen to the cynics, the gossips, and those who take threads of the truth and double down, having a field day spreading untruths. Look past the errors, shut down the rumor mill, see who God created in them, and be part of the truth—speaking into their life so they too can believe they are who God created them to be. It changes them, and it will change you too.

Chapter Nine

Jesus and the Broken

H ave you ever been broken? As you have turned the pages of this book, could you relate? Maybe you have been where Jeremy or my friends were, on the other side of the broken, being broken. Either way, some form of brokenness will always bring us to our knees. Brokenness is a hard, desperate space to be, where you are simply looking for the solace for your sorrow, the salve to your bane. Yet when we realize that Jesus is there through it all, sees it all, knows our hearts, and is that salve—that solace—it has a wild way of changing us for the better, teaching us to live with a different lens. This lens is a zeal for His name to be known, transforming the way we see people and encounter them. It catapults us into passionately sharing the gospel through our words and actions however we can.

I refer to the account of the woman at the well quite often, as it is the one I most relate to in all of scripture. It also reveals so much of the character and kindness of Jesus that it draws me nearer and nearer to Him. She was an outcast, an outsider, and she was broken. He was a rescuer, a lover, a balm to the broken.

It was then that they met. She encountered Him like she'd never encountered anything in her life.

This was a woman who had made some terrible choices in her life, had been with many men, and had pretty much been marked with a scarlet letter. So much so that she would go to get water at the well in the hottest times of day, when it would be most painful to carry those heavy jars home. She did this to avoid the gawking, the rumor mill, and whatever awful critiques were probably shouted at her.

Do you hear that? The physical pain of carrying heavy jars of water in the greatest heat of the day was less to her than the emotional pain of judgment and gossip. She was choosing the physical discomfort over the emotional agony. Let that sink in.

Then we read that the Savior of the World went to her. He went out of His way to go to her. He did what He wasn't supposed to do, breaking all kinds of boundaries to do it. A Jew should never have been speaking to a Samaritan, a man should never have been speaking to this woman one-on-one, and the list goes on. Yet, Jesus did. He did not care about her reputation; He did not worry about her status or how it looked. He cared about the state of her soul. He wanted this woman to experience the hope He had, the living water.

Jesus knew exactly when she'd be there, and He knew exactly how broken she was. There He was to meet her. Just as He knows us and knows exactly where to meet us in our brokenness.

I often think about what her mindset was that day and every day as she walked to the well. Was her head down as she made the journey, just hoping and praying she wouldn't see anyone? Was she hoping she wouldn't feel the stares or hear the gossip? Did she imagine that her life would always be like this? Did she wake up every single day dreading the journey to attain the jugs of water necessary to live? She knew it was something that couldn't be avoided, but maybe she tried to figure out a different way. Those staring couldn't see their own brokenness through all her issues that they presumed worse than theirs.

Did she hope for a change or a way to fix herself, but not know if she'd ever find it? She'd heard of the coming Messiah, but did she truly believe He would give her all she needed and transform her life?

When He said to her, "I, the one speaking to you, am he" (John 4:26 NIRV), what was that first moment of freedom like for her? Was it the first time in her life that she felt like she could breathe and lift her head high? Did she feel the chains breaking off all the things she'd been carrying and ashamed of?

I thought I knew Jesus for all He was before I made the bad decisions I did. But, I did not. It wasn't until those quiet moments just after everything was uncovered, my head hanging low and my soul abounding in brokenness, that I met my Savior's eyes like never before. His gaze transfixed on me, and as with the woman at the well, He boldly proclaimed over my life that He was who He said He was. He was the Messiah, the Living Water, the Good Shepherd, Jehovah Rapha.

Friend, He is that good, meeting us right where we are. In the middle of all of our brokenness, there He stands. In the middle of the heat blazing on our scorched souls as we try to carry the things we think will quench our thirst, as the woman at the well did and as I did, He is there, extending the grace and mercy of His living water that will fill our deepest, driest wells.

When that miraculous healing takes place, we cannot do anything but turn toward His freedom and run hard to tell the world of His greatness. It spurs us to leave the broken things behind and live anew. It is an interesting thing that happens in someone when they have met the pit of darkness and then been kissed by the radiance of a Savior. When we are brought from death to life, dark to light, it is a holy transformation that we cannot hide. When you go from hiding, secrets, and shame to victory, freedom, and joy, people will see the new you and want to know how it happened. (Never mind the naysayers, doubting Debbies, and no-matter-what criticizers. I have learned that people won't change until they themselves have truly experienced Jesus.)

I'm so thankful God can and will use the broken. Let that be an encouragement to you today.

There are marked encounters in my story that I had with those who have had miraculous transformations in their own lives. These are those who looked beyond the pain they felt from me, because they'd been there in their own ways, and *immediately* lived out love. It is shocking to receive, but a blessing beyond measure.

One of the very first was my mother-in-law. When I was sitting at the table in her home, confessing what I had done to her son, she didn't stop rubbing my back and consoling me. It was a physical symbol of compassion despite unfaithfulness. As I concluded my confession, with tears in her eyes, she stared right back at me and instantly said, "You are still the little girl I prayed for for my son, and I love you."

What? How? It is unbelievable, astounding, and beautiful, that kind of love. To receive it is remarkable. Only through the love of Jesus Christ could someone stare into the face of another who had just broken their heart, or even worse, broken their child's heart, and say what she said. Only a person who has experienced the miraculous work of a Savior in their own life could extend this kind of grace and compassion instantaneously.

I am a better woman for it.

A dear friend of mine, Mel, had a similar response. I'd become close to her after teaching her daughter years earlier in the student ministry at our church. We sat outside on a beautiful sunny day eating lunch together as I confessed the not-so-sunny things I'd done. Her heart clearly grieved, sorrow filling her face as tears escaped from her eyes. Yet there she sat, looking me in the eyes as she proclaimed that she still loved me as her friend. She expressed her hurt over what I had done, but in the next breath exclaimed that she was still thankful for the way I'd ministered to her daughter years earlier in our Sunday school class. She reminded me that God had still used me. My choices of late did not negate how God had worked.

She loved me even still. She saw me for who God created me to be, despite what I had done in the meantime.

I am a better woman for it.

In the middle of my affair, as the depths of sin took a toll on my appearance and body, another friend boldly walked up to me one Sunday with an intensity in her eyes. She looked me dead in the face and said, "Something is wrong with you, and I can't ignore it anymore. Let me help you." Tears began falling from my eyes as I hugged her neck and said, "Thank you, but I'm good," and then walked away. I didn't speak to her from that day onward, avoiding her at all costs because I imagined she'd catch on, and I desperately didn't want that. I knew it hurt her that I did that. When everything came out and the news made it to her, I received a text. Her message to me said, "I knew something was wrong that day, and now I know what it was, but it doesn't change what I said. Let me help you because I love you." This was a woman who had faced betrayal, death, and so much else in her life, and in the midst of it all, she also experienced Jesus making a way for her to extend that same love to me.

I am a better woman for it.

These are just a few examples of the beautiful ways that those who had truly experienced brokenness and healing through Jesus in their own lives displayed His love to me. How someone could see these encounters and not be changed is beyond my comprehension.

Let me acknowledge that not everyone will respond as these did. I most certainly did not get that response from all of my family and friends, and when I didn't, I understood that the person was hurt and in pain. In those moments, remember that our God always extends grace when others don't.

In the same way that I had encounters with followers of Christ, the woman at the well encountered our Rescuer-Redeemer, and it miraculously transformed her life. It was evident from the start. I believe that unmistakable transformation started being visible first when the disciples appeared before she even ran away. As they approached and saw what was happening, they knew it would have been odd for Jesus, a Jewish man, to be communicating with a woman in public like that. But scripture tells us none of them said a word, none of them questioned it. Personally, I believe they saw the undeniable change in this woman; they saw the hope beaming from her and knew the miracle that had just taken place. (Excuse me for taking liberties there, but I really do think the disciples saw the change in her, and that might quite possibly be why they didn't question Him speaking to her.)

After this, she ran into town, facing the people who once had disdain for her. She simply said, "Come, see" (John 4:29), and they went! They saw the difference and they went! They could see Him through her before they even saw Him. This was because the chains had been broken, the shame lifted, the hope restored. She had experienced Jesus.

I experienced Jesus through His people and thus began the transformation in my own life, and now I can't stop proclaiming the hope of a Savior. I ran into His arms, the life He had made for me, leaving behind the things that would always leave me thirsty, wanting more, and never filling the gaping hole in my life. I experienced Jesus.

When the Creator of the World meets you in your brokenness, it changes you in the most extraordinary ways. It opens your eyes and your heart to live in a way you never have before. There was a time when I would have scoffed at those who walked the same path I did. I would have gossiped, judged, and turned my back on anyone who did anything remotely close to what I did.

Today, that is different. My first reaction when I hear of someone who has found themselves in a dark and desperate pit is to grieve for them. My heart breaks, and I immediately pray for the redemption and freedom that they can only find through Jesus. Then, I extend compassion and kindness in whatever capacity I can. This only happens because they are what was extended to me through our God and His people, and I understand the deep impact they have on one's soul.

Until you have experienced Jesus in your own brokenness, it is hard to comprehend.

Jesus and the broken: a remarkable thing. Jesus and the broken: a regular thing in scripture. Jesus and the broken: He heals, He transforms, He redeems.

Chapter Ten

Hidden Healing

At the point of explosion, when everything came out, my schedule emptied quickly as my job was lost and many friends went silent. I found myself sitting at my kitchen table day in and day out, just crying. Each morning, I would hold myself together long enough to get my boys off to school and my husband off to work, and then I would go sit, reading scripture, journaling my heart's cries, and weeping. Gazing out our big kitchen window from time to time, all I could muster up the strength to say was "Oh, Jesus." That simple phrase was the only speech that would escape my lips. It was as though every other word in my vocabulary was paralyzed except the word Jesus.

I desperately wanted the "how-to" manual to get out of this mess and get out fast. I wanted quick-fix steps to remedy my own soul and my husband's heart and make everyone around me forgive and trust me again. Could I find this at the local bookshop in the self-help section? Was there a YouTube video on it? The answer to that is a solid no.

Quick fixes simply mask an issue; they never remedy the source and only lead to more destruction in the future. True solutions only come from the gospel of Jesus Christ and are a process of heart transformation stemming from full surrender, blended with grace and mercy gifted through the redeeming love of our Savior.

In our brokenness, we must seek Him and surrender.

This entire process begins with total confession to the Lord. Until that step happens, nothing else will succeed, and you cannot walk freely in the light of our Savior. Darkness will remain like the steady clouds on a rainy day. The heaviness of holding it all in, otherwise known as self-preservation, is a weighty and unnecessary burden. Admitting to every piece of sin and leaving nothing unsaid is the only way to break free, mend the mess, and fully heal.

Once I emptied every bit of me, confessing even the ugliest of uglies, the Lord slowly began His work. No sugarcoating here, and just repeating what's already been said because I want it known that it is a very painful process. It can be likened to slowly pulling off a band-aid, only this is a band-aid over your embattled and scarred soul. At times it can seem as though you can't breathe or take another minute of it all, and there are moments where sleep is the only reprieve.

I remember a time when it was so painful that I just wanted the day to hurry so I could crawl into bed and beg the Lord to help me fall asleep so that for just a few hours I wouldn't have to think about anything. I could forget all the wretched things I'd done. I could forget how deeply I had hurt my husband and everyone around me. I didn't have to think about everyone who hated my guts. Sleep was the only pardon some days.

However, part of this process is enduring the pain, pushing through, and clinging to life through Jesus. I had finally grasped the concept of fully clinging to the Almighty because, frankly, I had nothing else to cling to but Him.

Once your soul is bared, the Lord can come in and fill those wounded, sinful places with the trappings of His goodness. 1 John 1:9 confirms this: "If we confess our sins, he is faithful and righteous to forgive us our sins and to cleanse us from all unrighteousness." He is forever faithful, even in our unfaithful moments. His love poured out cleanses us of our wicked ways. What a gift He graciously lavishes on us.

Even in the moments when I found myself confessing, broken, and barely holding on, there were finally glimmers of peace. It was such a peculiar place to be: My life was in complete shambles, yet at the same time, I had finally found peace, a peace I am unsure I had ever felt before. This peace was as pure as freshly laid snow, untouched on a still morning. However, amidst the peace, there was still much work to be done.

When we surrender and allow the Lord to enter into our hearts and heal us, we still have consequences to endure, pain to wrestle through, and feelings to navigate and unpack. Our God isn't a genie; we can't rub His belly and see all things instantly changed and everything magically made better. That, my friend, is what we would call cheap grace. What is harder—but most victorious—is having Him carry us through, sustaining us as we live it all out. This is true, glorious, miraculous grace.

As the days went on, I peeled back layer upon layer of my shattered and damaged heart. It was in those very moments that I felt myself being drawn closer to the Lord than I have ever known in my life. It was in those instances that I began to grasp what grace and mercy truly are and what Christ had done for me on the cross. It was in those quiet moments at my kitchen table that I finally heard the Lord saying to me, "I love you, my child, you are mine." I am certain that I could not have heard Him speak this to me before this very moment because there was too much chaos and disorder drowning the whispers of my Savior. The truths I heard out of these whispers were:

- I am His child.

- He loves me in spite of it all.

- He will rescue me.

- He is my refuge.

I had finally allowed the Lord to come in and be the ruler of my heart, filling my entire being to the brim with Him. My heart was only fed with the nourishment of His truth straight from the scriptures. Each day I read and also wrote out the words of Psalm 46. It was my everyday solace.

God is our refuge and strength, a helper who is always found in times of trouble. Therefore we will not be afraid, though the earth trembles and the mountains topple into the depths of the seas, though its waters roar and foam and the mountains quake with its turmoil. Selah

[There is] a river—its streams delight the city of God, the holy dwelling place of the Most High. God is within her; she will not be toppled. God will help her when the morning dawns. Nations rage, kingdoms topple; the earth melts when He lifts His voice. The Lord of Hosts is with us; the God of Jacob is our stronghold. Selah

Come, see the works of the Lord, who brings devastation on the earth. He makes wars cease throughout the earth. He shatters bows and cuts spears to pieces; He burns up the chariots. "Stop [your fighting]—and know that I am God, exalted among the nations, exalted on the earth." The Lord of Hosts is with us; the God of Jacob is our stronghold. Selah.

What beauty there is in the safe place of our strong and mighty God. Even when the troubled times are present, He is here. He is right here among the chaos, among the ruins; our God is our constant.

Our God undeniably is our refuge when we are in murky waters. Take hold of Him. These moments in our lives will find us weak; they will cause us to be frail and break us to the point where we are defenseless on our own. Nevertheless, He is our strength. Trust in Him.

There is a river whose streams delight the city of God. As Gaebelein's commentary states, "This river is a metaphor of blessing and restoration." May we purify ourselves in the river of the Most High, allowing it to flow through us to the waters of rebuilding the damage we have done in ourselves and in others. Let Him cleanse.

Our God is in us; therefore, it is impossible to fail. He graciously gives us new mercies each morning. These new mercies allow us to breathe afresh each day, even when the wars of sorrow and despair have overtaken us the day before. Rest in Him.

Everything else falls away when He speaks, and nothing will have victory over the spoken word of our God.

We must be still, we must stop fighting our own battles. Instead, lay them at His feet; bring your burdens, your mess, the disarray of life to Him, and let Him enter in and restore your heart's home. He is the Almighty. He is with us. He is our fortress.

As a journey from restoration to redemption is traveled, what glorious promises we can find woven into these beautiful writings from God's Word. This is just a snippet of the assurances we can rest in. The only how-to book on the shelves worthy of reading and seeking answers from is the Bible itself. The only trustworthy, true remedies that will never change or need to improve with the times are found in the words of our Lord. The only thing able to breathe new life into you and the relationships you have is Him.

No matter the type of betrayal, disloyalty, or mistrust that has soured a relationship, it can only be remedied and healed through our God. The most important place for healing and redemption is at His feet, righting our relationship with Him. All other facets of this painful process pale in comparison with the making new that only He can do.

Scripture gives me the answers when I am asked, as I often am, "How do you forgive yourself?" For some, the answer to that question seems unimaginable, totally impossible. Many think their sins are unforgivable, but there is One who does not. His name is Jesus Christ. Over and over, scripture tells us He died for *all* of our sins. I have to believe what He says about me in scripture to forgive myself.

For Christ also suffered for sins once for all, the righteous for the unrighteous, that He might bring you to God, after being put to death in the fleshly realm but made alive in the spiritual realm. (1 Peter 3:18)

He Himself bore our sins in His body on the tree, so that, having died to sins, we might live for righteousness; by His wounding you have been healed. (1 Peter 2:24)

Love consists in this: not that we loved God, but that He loved us and sent His Son to be the propitiation for our sins. (1 John 4:10)

For I passed on to you as most important what I also received: that Christ died for our sins according to the Scriptures. (1 Corinthians 15:3)

It doesn't say some sin or just these particular sins; it is for all. This is where I knew how and why I had to forgive myself. By not forgiving myself after confessing and surrendering, I was saying, "Jesus, what You did on the cross wasn't enough for me." This is one of the biggest things that I hope you take away from this book. Remember it, take hold of it, and live it out.

I sat in shame and guilt for a long while, deeply questioning how I could dare forgive myself for the heinous things I had done. If you are doing the same, sitting in the shame of your sin, whatever it is, you aren't taking hold of the forgiveness He shed His blood for. Through the act of not forgiving yourself, you are telling the Savior of the Earth that it wasn't enough, when indeed it is all you need. He died for you, dear friend. Step into the freedom His poured-out blood has given you. Repent, surrender, and live out the freedom set before you. Recognize the depths of love the Rescue Redeemer demonstrated for you, and don't look back. Freedom in forgiveness is like a soothing sonnet singing healing over your soul.

It isn't lost on me that in our humanness, this is easier said than done. There are severe consequences one can face in their sin, which can include memories, unlearning behaviors, trauma, and so many other things. That is where the practical steps of this process come in.

My number-one, highly recommended, non-negotiable practical step that should be taken from the moment of impact is finding a solid, biblically based licensed counselor. This is someone to whom you can fully empty every ill feeling, bad thought, and sinful desire. A person who will acknowledge your struggle but won't let you sit in it. Someone who has the training and ability to speak the truth while understanding the reality of what it is you are navigating. When we combine the practical realm with the spiritual realm, miraculous things can happen.

All of the work I had done at my kitchen table with the Lord coincided with me sitting on my counselor's couch. All of it was only done through my surrender and fiercely fighting for it through the work of a great Redeemer.

One of the safest places I found in those early days of healing was sitting in the office of my counselor. It wasn't what you would imagine, or at least what I had imagined, a therapy office to be. I always pictured them as being sterile and comfortable, not cozy. That did describe the office of the first counselor Jeremy and I went to, where we had that very bizarre experience. However, the office of the dear counselor we landed with was warm, inviting, and filled with peace. The room was soft-lit with lamps instead of hard, piercing overhead bulbs. The shelves were filled with books, God's Word, picture frames of sweet affirmations, and delicate flowers throughout. The counselor herself was a kind, gentle soul, a beautiful gift sent from the Lord.

She was someone who always looked at me with compassion, but also spoke to me with hard truths and matter-of-fact honesty. She also took me to the throne of Jesus every session, not ever ending our time together until she had prayed over me. I looked forward to my time with her each week, some days longing desperately to be on that couch, looking into the eyes of genuine care and concern, pouring out my heart in that secure space.

Our finding her was God-ordained and a precious piece in the puzzle of redemption. Three times a week for many months, I found myself sitting across from her. That is a lot, you might think, but let me tell you: When God is on a rescue, restore, and redeem mission with a soul, it is vital to exhaust all avenues of help He provides. While He can do anything on His own, He also provides physical tools to help us along the way. They are imperative.

When we are broken and on spiritual life support, redemption looks so far off. All we can see from the point of view of our own exploding lives is the fragments of ourselves and others who were caught in the line of fire, lying all over the floor. Oftentimes, the restoration of our lives doesn't even seem possible at that moment. Yet, that is right where it starts. It starts on the floor, wallowing in the chaos we have created and then getting up, and emptying all the turmoil and disarray out of our beings.

I will go to my grave emphatically saying that healing will *not* come unless you empty yourself wholly, completely, of it all! Every single bit, the lies, the deceit, the most awful of awfuls you dare not speak: Speak it. Don't try and self-preserve, don't deflect, don't tuck a few things away thinking you can't ever confess *that*. Nope, don't do it. That is what the enemy wants you to do. He wants you to withhold a few things because you believe the lie that this particular thing can't ever get out, that it will doom you forever. What will doom you forever is holding it in. Holding it in is hindering healing. Soon, it will fester, take root again, and bloom another garden of gunk that you'll end up having to wade through a second time. Clean it out, let it all out, empty yourself.

One of the freest moments of my journey, but also the most painful and humiliating, was the moment of truth. The moment I could look Jeremy and those closest to me in the eye and speak with total and complete honesty. Was it painful? You betcha! It was the most painful thing I have ever had to do in my entire life and something I never want to have to do again. But it was absolutely, unequivocally the moment that my journey turned towards restoration. There was no holding back; it all came out. It was the poison in my body, rotting my soul to a depraved state, finally being relinquished. The poison would soon turn to purity.

That poison came out, and the cleansing living water of a holy God rushed in. My soul has never felt refreshment like it did in those days. It was washed white as snow, made new, fresh. It was a clean palette for the Lord to now do His work. It was freedom.

At the one-year mark of seeing my counselor, she looked at me and said, "My work is done." I was alarmed! No, it was not. I needed her! I immediately said, "Wait a minute, I can't stop seeing you now!" She assured me I could. She was the training wheels of the restored-and-redeemed process. For a year she was an anchor for me, holding me while I learned to move forward again, equipping me with tools for my mind, my heart, and my soul. A year later, she saw in me what I hadn't seen yet. She saw the changing tide, the transforming movement, and was confident in my ability to keep healing, keep moving, and keep allowing the Lord to do His work. It was her time to step aside.

She told me how proud she was of me. She expressed her confidence in the work I had put in and my ability to keep going without her. She even told me she admired me and was certain that the Lord was going to use my story in miraculous ways one day. I politely nodded but was also thinking to myself, "Yeah, right." I left that day afraid, but holding onto her confidence in me. God used that precious woman in mighty, and extraordinary ways in that year with her.

It took some adjusting, not having my time in the counselor's office to look forward to. But I replaced it with more time in God's Word or an encouraging book or a Bible study. At this point, I was beginning to breathe easier and felt a smidgeon of growth in myself, all because of Jesus.

One of the most precious gifts in my time in my counselor's office was when I recalled something that had happened just before I embarked on the affair. It is crazy how these things happen through healing—something I'd long forgotten about bubbled up in the process, bringing a life lesson I didn't quite expect. It is not a story I have shared before because I recognize that some may not fully believe it. I also believe I will come under some scrutiny for this, and some may say it is bogus, but I wholly believe it is what happened and am willing to risk the ridicule.

I was at our Good Friday service, one of my favorite services we would hold at church. A cross sat in the middle of the worship center with chairs rearranged to gather around it, as lights dimly lit the room. It was a service filled with incredible worship, and there was always this sense of nearness to our Savior like no other. The presence of the Holy Spirit was all-encompassing.

As worship began on that particular evening, I was overwhelmed to the point of sobbing. While tears will often fall from my eyes during worship, this was different. This was an uncontrollable weeping that I could not stop. At one point, I had to excuse myself so as not to be a distraction. I had no other explanation except that worship simply overcame me like it never had before.

I left the service that night baffled by what had happened. I was puzzled by it, unable to discern what had happened because my heart and soul were already clouded by deception and lies. It wouldn't be until much later that I would understand. With healing, reflection, and growth, it all made sense, and I could grasp what had happened that night.

You see, this Good Friday service was merely days before the final step into the affair was taken. I had already begun justifying, turning away, and ignoring the warnings of the Lord. Those catch-in-your-spirit moments that happen when you are walking with the Lord in freedom? I wasn't sensing them, because my soul had already taken the path to destruction. So, in that moment of sorrow that night, I believe my reaction was the weeping of the Holy Spirit grieving for me.

Ephesians 4:30 says, "And don't grieve God's Holy Spirit, who sealed you for the day of redemption." When we do anything that is in contradiction to the Holy Spirit's nature, it grieves Him. When we dishonor, disparage, or are disobedient, the Spirit mourns.

At that point, I had fully surrendered myself to what was to come. I had turned away from the Almighty and turned toward a sinful path. The Holy Spirit knew that and grieved it, and His sorrow overwhelmed me even though I was too blinded in that moment to realize.

The Holy Spirit is so personal it is mind-blowing. The Spirit is a gift given to us by a God who loves us deeply. He provided us with the Holy Spirit to help us in our walk with Him each day. When we go against that, His heart is broken and He is grieved.

What this revelation did for me was show me that I need to be walking so close to the Lord that I can sense that grief, that sorrow from the Holy Spirit, immediately and change my course in response. Part of growing deeper in our relationship with the Lord, living more like Jesus each day, is being sensitive to the Spirit that lives within us.

Today, I can say it is evident to me when I mess up, choose wrong, or act a fool. I become so uncomfortable that I instantly know something isn't right. When I am talking to the Lord each day, my prayer is that He never let me lose my sensitivity to the Spirit again. I pray that I never turn so far that everything becomes clouded and I become clueless.

The intimacy with our Savior that we have been gifted through the Holy Spirit is sacred. The relationship we have with our Redeemer is holy. When we find ourselves in spaces of brokenness, He is standing right there waiting on us. He welcomes us back home with open arms, letting love, compassion, and hope rain down on us like never before. Navigating the waters of redemption can only be traveled successfully when we begin surrendering to Him.

The hidden healing with our Jehovah Jireh is the most important aspect of healing. It is hidden because it happens in the hallowed moments with just you and Him. It is for no one else but you and Him. It is not to be put on display; it is not to be shared with anyone else. Solely you and solely Him; nothing else matters. The more we lean into His love, the more we will know His heart.

Chapter Eleven

Brokenness Bears Beauty

B roken pieces were shattered everywhere, shrapnel sprayed near and far, the waves of hurt and pain crashing down on so many. Then, all of it, every single bit of it, was gathered, brought to a place of beauty, mended, and made new. The old has gone, newness has come, and freedom is ringing. Our God, the waymaker, delights in restoring us and rejoices when His people link arms with the broken, encouraging this process to fulfillment.

When everything fell apart, I was certain God would never use me again. It seemed nearly impossible that I could ever enter the realm of ministry or even point people to Jesus in any way because I was a fraud. That is exactly where the enemy wanted me to live and die. He wanted me defeated and hopeless so I would give up and abandon the life of being a follower of Jesus altogether. That is his end goal with all of us, the last link in his chains of false victory. Thankfully, it was not my endgame, because Jesus rescued me and used His people to breathe life into my soul.

Scripture is filled with countless examples of how God rescues broken vessels and uses them to carry His message to the masses. One of His greatest tools to use in the rescue operation is His own people. Isn't that just the beauty of who He is? When our God is welcomed into a messy broken place, He will restore it to new and use it for His glory. That is displayed clearly in the words of 2 Corinthians 5:17: "Therefore if anyone is in Christ, there is a new creation; old things have passed away, and look, new things have come!" He does indeed make all things new! There is nothing more beautiful than a story of restoration: from ashes to glory, from graves to gardens, from death to life—redemption.

Paul, before he knew Jesus, was a zealous Pharisee who sought to persecute any and all followers of Christ. His first entrance into scripture is at the stoning of Stephen in Acts 7:8.

In the very next chapter of Acts, he begins to ravage the church, going from house to house and putting people in prison. Then in Acts 9, Paul goes to the high priest asking for letters to the synagogues at Damascus to begin persecuting any Christians he encounters. As he set out on the road to Damascus, he was on a mission not only to destroy the church, but to completely annihilate it. On that road, Paul had an encounter with God, and his entire life was transformed, completely altering the track of Paul's being from death to life! Paul immediately became a defender of the faith and started his journey of preaching the gospel. God transforms His people, and in my opinion, no man had a greater impact on the kingdom of God than Paul did. Doesn't that just energize your socks off and make you want to shout from the rooftops what a mighty, extraordinary God we serve? I cannot wait to meet him in heaven. Next to Jesus, please let me find Paul ASAP on the day I arrive. Are there restraining orders in heaven?

Rahab was a prostitute who lived in Jericho. She was popular for lodging and entertaining travelers. Get my drift there? She chose to help two spies who came to her home to hide from the king. Her one condition in hiding them was that when Jericho was invaded by the Israelites, she and her family were to be spared. In Joshua 2:11, Rahab says, "The Lord your God is God in heaven above and on earth below," indicating to many theologians a confession of faith.

While I am no theologian, I too believe that was indicative of Rahab knowing our God. When the invasion came, Joshua ordered the two spies to go save Rahab and her family. She was rescued by God's people and had a home among the nation of Israel. She was rescued and redeemed, and in the first chapter of the book of Matthew, you will find her name written in the lineage of Jesus. Go look right now, I promise it'll make your heart leap with joy! No seriously, don't pass this nugget by; she was part of the ancestry of Jesus Christ. Oh, how He loves us. He stops at nothing, even enlisting His people to be part of the process. Isn't it just overwhelming what the Savior of the World does for us, in us, and through us?

He equips us with the courage and peace to endure it all. John 16:33 says, "I have told you these things so that in Me you may have peace. You will have suffering in this world. Be courageous! I have conquered the world." Our peace in every situation only comes from Him. As Gaebelein writes, "Even in the hour of his greatest suffering he had an unshakable confidence in the victorious purpose of God." We will most definitely have trouble in this world. We will have our own hours of great suffering, but He has overcome the world, and we can rest in the promise that God's purpose in it all is victorious. When we are smothered by the ashes of our messes, Jesus Christ comes to redeem us and carry us to victory. When we are smothered by the ashes of someone else's mess, Jesus Christ comes to renew us and gives us the strength to face it, overcome it, and oftentimes be part of the salvage crew carrying that someone else to victory.

I could write this entire chapter simply on examples woven through scripture of the promises of His redeeming love to broken people, all indicative of how our God never ever wants us to sit in the soot of sorrow alone forever. He wants nothing more than for the ashes and the brokenness of our lives to be brought to newness and beauty. He wants nothing less than His very best for each and every one of us. He desires for us all to be in this together as His people, supporting and uplifting each other through every chapter of our lives.

As the seasons in our lives go by, there are moments when we feel like we can and probably need to put a period on a particular season. Often we want that period to be bold and engraved, to make it clear that it is in fact the end. Maybe an exclamation point is better at times to express the end of a hard chapter, but one that has an exciting, thrilling, life-filled ending. An ending that is the beginning of a brand-new, hope-filled chapter.

This very chapter in this book that you are reading right this minute is the exclamation point: the point where the brokenness of my life bore the beauty of Jesus Christ. This is the culmination of all the pain, all the heartache, and all the hurt being used for the glory of our God. Sometimes, it may seem like He isn't near. In fact, it may take a long time to get to the point where you see the beauty with your own eyes, but it never means that He isn't working. He never pauses, and He never leaves us. Some parts of this goodness, we may not ever see here on this earth; they may be waiting for us in eternity. While that is sometimes a hard pill to swallow, it is a truth we must trust. Life is a process of stripping the old and dead and waiting for the goodness of the fruits to bloom.

When we aren't cultivating our relationship with the Lord and allowing Him to work in our lives, we are instead allowing sin to come in and overtake our hearts and our minds, swallowing up the splendor of who Jesus has created us to be.

When this happens, we get so lost in the thick of it, we can't tell the good from the bad. We are unable to navigate the path that our God has laid out for us. It is at that point that we enter into a dark wintery season where everything not of Him must die. Our being remains, with breath still in our lungs, but we are clinging to life through Him, the only good and right thing about us. At this moment, every other thing about us must be stripped away, and some branches may even need to be broken off completely, leaving us in what seems like bitter cold, barren, and empty. What a brutal way to think of it, I know. Yet, what a glaring image of what actually has to happen for us to be redeemed and restored to the way the Lord would have us.

At this point of bitter cold and emptiness, we surround ourselves with Him, His Word, and His people, each playing a vital role in our journey back to wholeness. Through all of this nourishment, spring is near. As we heal, growing and dwelling in the goodness of God and His people, new life will bloom. Those blooms radiate His goodness, and we, in turn, radiate the glory of our God as we grow in His love. We can simply dwell in the beauty of Him.

*"Glory follows afflictions, not as the day follows the night but as the spring
follows the winter; for [as] the winter prepares the earth for the spring, so
do afflictions sanctified prepare the soul for glory."*
—*Richard Sibbes*

Brokenness can only bear the beauty of Jesus when the steps of
restoration have been lived out according to His Word. No fast track
to repair exists. But what can make this process exceptionally beautiful
is when those who have been betrayed come alongside the betrayer in
spite of wounded hearts and broken trust, coming together to wrestle
through the mess and ashes to get to the splendor. God's glory is revealed
in magnificent ways when this occurs. I saw this through my spouse's
steadfast love, my family's unwavering affection, my friends' commitment to remain, and even my church's pledge to endure the battle with
me. What majesty explodes when this all transpires!

That precious husband I spoke of, and whom you had the privilege of
hearing from in Chapter Four, indeed stayed the course, never wavering,
not one bit. He has been my champion on the entire path to redemption.
Even little details, things you'd never realize carried weight, are significant. For many years of our marriage, Jeremy would send me off for a
night stay by myself in a hotel to relax. Alone time is my jam, and this was
a simple reprieve for me that always filled my cup. I abused that privilege
in the midst of the affair, and so in our healing, I never asked for it. I
didn't think it was a good idea. Recently, as I was concluding a very busy
and exhaustive ministry weekend, he looked at me and said, "I booked
you a night at a hotel on the oceanfront. Go relax and enjoy." That was

more than a kind gesture; that was a bold statement saying, "I love you, I trust you, and I am for you."

I can declare to you today: That man is my best friend and my safe place. The Lord has worked in miraculous ways, making a broken marriage that was limping along more radiant than any star I've ever seen in the sky. Our good God has breathed new life into our relationship, building a bond between us that is unrivaled. Two people with determined obedience to the Savior of the World, in return, are rescued, made new, and living a life to glorify the God of the Universe in every way. Even more, as empty nesters now, we are most certainly living our best life! God is so, so good.

Those friends who kept ringing my doorbell, sending me emails, and praying over me—all the best friends a girl could ever ask for—lived out loyalty in the face of my disloyalty, and they are more precious than gold. They are few, and they are treasured. These are friends who speak truth, strengthen you, strengthen your bond with them, and most importantly with Jesus. Proverbs 27:17: "As iron sharpens iron, so one person sharpens another." "Constructive criticism between friends develops character," in the words of Gaebelein's commentary. I can only hope that I would do the same in return as each of these prized women has done for me.

I have even seen glimpses of goodness in friends who I had not been able to speak to in years. I was standing in the same place that I do every Sunday morning at church as I welcome people, answer questions, and help wherever necessary. I glanced over my shoulder, and there she was: an old friend whom I had not spoken to in over eight years. As I watched her get closer and closer, everything about our last interaction came rushing back to my mind. This was someone who had been struck by the shrapnel of my reckless words and bad decisions. All those years ago, hateful talk had been exchanged, and promises were declared that we would never speak again.

Yet here we were, years later, facing each other for the first time. As she passed by, I smiled and raised my hand to wave. She looked away and kept walking. My heart sank. I was so saddened and confused by that response I convinced myself it wasn't her, because how could she just walk by and not even say "hi" after all these years?

An hour later, as I was standing in the very same place, she passed by again, but this time she stopped and smiled. At that moment, everything that happened eight years previous faded away. It was as though the Lord washed His goodness right over us as we stood there, renewing and refreshing us for a new day.

This friend was one whom I had continued to pray for throughout the years. I had asked the Lord year after year if this relationship could ever be redeemed. Not one glimmer of hope was on the horizon, and I had accepted that our redemption would be in eternity. That is, until that sweet Sunday.

A few days later, we met for coffee, apologies were offered from both of us, stories were shared, and a new friendship bloomed fresh. Sitting across from me, she shared how she could *see* the new person I was. She went on to say that my love for the Lord and all He had done in my life was so evident. Oh, how Jesus is so, so good.

Oh, and that church that carried us along throughout the entire restoration process? Yeah, that one that I worked for but was fired from because of my poor choices. That very church chose to stay by my side and be a part of the entire journey. That same place opened its arms with willing hearts, mouths filled with truth, love-woven words, and took each step with me. There is no greater picture of the gospel. Now, years later, the story lives on in all of its splendor.

This incredible team worked hard with me, carried me through the hard places, poured out abundant grace, and then brought me back on staff. Not only was I brought back on staff, I was raised into leadership, leading the Women's Ministry for several years. This wasn't an end goal for me. This wasn't what I expected in restoration, because restoration was about becoming who God created me to be, restoring me as a wife and as a mom. This was not a wiggle-my-nose, all is kumbaya, and they trust me again situation.

This was the fruit of years of rebuilding and renewing. This was one small step at a time, living in obedience and humility. I still sit weepy-eyed and overwhelmed that this is my reality. God is so, so good. This was not an easy process or a short one. It was painful, hard, at times excruciating, but worth it all because of Jesus.

My turn to live out the same love that was bestowed on me is now here. The vibrant blooms of healthy growth are living out the affections of our Savior. The love and compassion given to me have spurred me to love and care for others in the same way. The Lord has given me many opportunities over the last several years to do just that.

When others have hurt me, I am no longer quick to shut them out. Yes, I confess, I was the most guilty of walking away when I felt hurt or betrayed. Yet no longer can I do that. No longer do I want to do that. Instead, I cling to the hope of a Savior as I pour out His love and compassion toward my offender. When a story of sorrow or a broken vessel enters my life, I count it a privilege to be able to navigate the mess with someone. It brings me joy to be able to speak the hope of Jesus into the depths of a hurting soul.

Friend, don't be fooled into thinking that my intent is to tell you that when you do everything right, all great things will happen. Don't miss me in that. That is not at all what my words are trying to convey. (Bye-bye, prosperity gospel, you have no place in truth.) What I am saying is that glimpses of goodness come out of hard spaces. I could write another book on all the devastation that came from this story. Sadly, that is the inevitable ugliness of sin. This book is simply a highlight reel of the glory of God that bloomed. These are the fruits that can come from God's people working together. My hope in pouring out every single word on these pages is that they can inspire and encourage those struggling to stay the course to, in fact, stay, with the help of a faithful God.

God sees you in those faithful moments. God will not forget the times when you stepped out in faith and loved in the hard spaces. What great assurance you can rest in, that the Lord is aware of every moment, every second. Be it as simple as the words that you speak or as great as the actions that you live out in love, He sees and knows it all. He will not forget your work and the love you showed in His name by serving the hurting. Hebrews 6:10 says, "For God is not unjust; he will not forget your work and the love you showed for his name when you served the saints—and you continue to serve them."

No small gesture, not even just a smile and nod of encouragement to someone, goes unnoticed. Amidst my chaos, I received a simple email saying how loved I was. Years later, it still brings tears to my eyes remembering it and the impact it had on my life. I just imagine the Lord sitting up in heaven, smiling down as He sees His people bring Him glory through their actions.

What if you lived and loved radically like our God in the midst of chaos and hurt? What if you could truly be the hands and feet of Jesus, having a heart like Jesus to stay the course in the midst of hurt? What if you could stay faithful in someone's faithless moments? What if we lived out 2 Timothy 2:13, "If we are faithless, He remains faithful, for He cannot deny himself," by remaining faithful like He does?

One of the definitions of the word *radical* is "favoring extreme changes in existing views, habits, conditions, or institutions." This explains loving like Jesus perfectly. To love like Jesus favors an extreme change from the love the world portrays. It sticks out. It is a completely different institution of love from any other. It is evident. It is undeniable. Radical love is Jesus' love.

The impact of living and loving radically goes beyond the person you are ministering to. It can reach outside the borders of that relationship, and frankly, that is part of its purpose. Others are watching and through your faithfulness can come to know our Savior. While someone's sin can cause a ripple effect of hurt, your kindness and faithfulness can cause a ripple effect of salvation. Doesn't that just blow your mind? It all leads back to how our God works all things, every single thing, for our good and His glory! Can you see the grandeur of our God here and how you can be a major part of that beauty? Souls can be saved and Jesus can be known through this radical living and loving.

To stay the course in the face of pain and mistrust is something the world shouts not to do. It is easier to believe that when the going gets tough, we should just move on, because the world screams that broken trust can never be repaired. To love in the face of hurt is to love in faith. When we choose to join the journey of redemption, we must believe that our God can lead our steps when we can't yet trust the untrusted. We have to trust Jesus enough to meet us in the mistrust.

I will never ever be able to express the gratitude I have for the circle of people who chose to stay the course with me. It brings tears to my eyes and joy to my heart when I think about it because I know beyond a shadow of a doubt that it was a hard choice. It was a painful choice, yet they did it anyway, and they brought glory to the King of Kings.

While this is a hard journey to sign up for, it can be a victorious one. I believe one of the highest callings God can ask of us is walking through the mud with someone. Choosing to be on the cleanup committee for a mess someone else made goes against every grain of our being. Especially when it is a mess where a little mud was slung your way and the hurt is still lingering. Jesus came and took on every speck of the mud in each of our lives, and He didn't just clean it up, He died for it.

Jesus loves us in spite of ourselves. Just like Jesus, we are called to love, even still.

Afterword

You may be wondering why I didn't mention much about that best friend, the other man's wife, whom I betrayed. I did that intentionally, as I wanted to be desperately careful to never hurt or offend her more. Just like Jeremy, she was the greatest victim in this story, and the deepest casualty in it all.

I wrote her a letter months after everything happened expressing my deepest sorrow and apologies for all that I did. I don't know if she ever read it, and that is completely understandable. Words could never express the regret I hold for the pain and trauma I caused her. To know that I may have triggered someone to question every friendship or relationship she ever had is soul-crushing. Someone should never have to experience or question that. My hope and prayer is that her heart has been mended and that the Lord brought newness and fresh, kind friendships to her in the wake of all that happened.

The bond and trust that friendships create between women should never be corrupted as ours was. The ultimate betrayal of friendship is what I did, and I own every bit of that. May she one day be able to hear and know the deep remorse that comes from the depths of my soul. May the God of the Universe help her know that our friendship did mean the world to me, and it wasn't all false. It's something so difficult to grasp. I, to this day, still believe that God brought her to me as a gift, a gift I ultimately wrecked. She is a beautiful soul, and the time we had was sweet before it was soured.

While I live in freedom today, that is one of the remaining areas where I cannot wait until heaven for the healing perfection to take place, a piece I long to experience of the glorious meeting of wholly healed souls in glory.

Even Still
A Poem of Rejoicing

you maybe wouldn't know it
if you looked at her today
and saw the shiny, happy pictures
that she put up on display

but if you lingered just a moment
and you read the words she typed
you would see a deeper image
than if you had only swiped

for the shiny, happy pictures
they are accurate and true
but they don't tell the fuller story
nor the journey she's been through

take this woman on a walk
and let her pour you some sweet tea
she will quickly take you deeper
to the bottom of the sea

where she wrecked a pretty life
and died upon that ocean floor
blew up everything she had
in grasping for that evil more

she was empty and unhappy
when she wandered from the narrow
never knowing just how deep
the whispered lies would pierce her marrow

but that's not the fuller picture
and it's not her journey's end
for she was rescued by a Hero
and revived by her best Friend

a Savior desperately was needed
and He heard her painful cries
with speed He came with love and kindness
and repentance filled her eyes

and now you know the simple truth
behind the joy you see in her
she once swam down into the depths
deserved the death that she incurred

but as He always, always does
He came and swam her to the surface
He will get the praise from now
because His glory is her purpose

all have wandered from the narrow
held tight to our evil will
but I am shattered by the truth
of how He loves us, even still

—Jodi Cowles

Acknowledgments

This book materialized out of a painful and destructive choice I made ten years ago and the aftermath of extraordinary and miraculous encounters that followed. Writing a book is a journey filled with challenges and triumphs, long days of wonder, weepy days of weary, and joy-filled days of success. It cannot be done alone, and I am deeply grateful to all who have supported me along the way.

Jeremy, you have been my steadfast companion throughout. Your unwavering love, patience, and compassion are unmatched. Your willingness to share our story, the pain to the victories, is a testament to who you are and your love for the Lord and his people. Thankful God gave me you.

To **my boys**, who are my greatest joy, and the biggest blessing in my life, I love you deeply.

To my **family** who stood with me through and through, I love you dearly and am eternally grateful for your endless love.

The **church** that stood with me, you exemplified what a community of faith should be. Thank you for your unwavering support and commitment to my restoration and redemption story. How you responded is unheard of in the church world, yet the very picture of the love of Jesus.

To my fiercest and closest **friends**, who stood by me through thick and thin, loving me despite everything—I am forever grateful for your presence in the depths of darkness and the heights of hope. As each of you read the stories I shared about you, I hope it will give you just a glimpse of the gratitude I have for your unending grace and love you have shown me.

To my mentors:

Donna, your unwavering love and friendship have been a constant source of strength. Your willingness to do whatever it took to carry me to the finish line and be who you saw me to be before I even could, leaves me undone each time I think about it. Thank you for doing life with me and never giving up on me. Let's go to Italy!

LG, your resilience and wisdom have lifted me up time and again. Thank you for speaking hard truths with gentle compassion and pouring out endless encouragement.

To my **prayer team**: your intercession before the throne of Jesus has sustained me throughout the writing process. Your prayers have been a powerful reminder of God's grace and provision.

Blue Hat Publishing: You were a true gift sent at just the right time. **Jodi**, my sweet book friend, who has become a lifetime friend, thank you for all the wisdom you poured out in this process, talking out ideas and helping chapters bloom. Also, dealing with my gamut of emotions on a regular basis and simply being a constant in this process is no small feat. You are beyond amazing.

Thank you all for believing in me and this project. You are what kept me going, even still.